1

The Science of Self-Learning:

How to Teach Yourself Anything, Learn More in Less Time, and Direct Your Own Education

By Peter Hollins,
Author and Researcher at
petehollins.com

Table of Contents

Chapter 1. Principles of Self-Learning

Most of us—or at least our parents—recall how education used to be in the 20th century, before technology made acquiring information super easy. We learned in institutionalized settings: the classroom, the laboratory, the workshop, and out in the field. We might have learned additional skills at trade schools or night classes. If you wanted to learn something, it required a lot of effort. Consider that encyclopedias used to be popular and widespread—because there was literally no other way of looking up information or learning by yourself. It almost feels like the dark ages when you realize how difficult it was to simply acquire knowledge and learn about what you're interested in.

In all of those stuffy traditional environments, someone else decided what we should learn beforehand, whether it was a school board, a private instructor, or family. Learning conferred a top-down relationship with someone else who had the knowledge we sought. Self-learning—in most, but not all, areas—wasn't considered as legitimate as getting an education from a known or accredited source. To enter professions or be considered in any positive light, you must have gone through the proper channels and received the pertinent pieces of paper that told people you were knowledgeable. Gatekeepers were everywhere and designed to keep you from rising.

The 21st century has changed all that, thank goodness. Self-education is a thriving industry. Students direct their own learning in topics that used to only be covered in college settings, and far beyond of course.

The Internet has opened up broad avenues of information access that are available to anyone with a connection. Somebody who truly wants to learn facts in history, science, the arts, business, technology, or literature can do so with at least a little comprehensiveness through online sources.

Students can supplement their traditional studies, or they can create their own curriculums designed to get them where they want to be. The business titans we worship these days don't even have the degrees that used to be required.

Still, self-education can seem like a grand undertaking. Indeed, it involves a higher personal drive and commitment than we had in our regimented school days because we're guiding ourselves when we self-learn. We're motivating ourselves. We're often learning in a vacuum, trying to derive meaning and knowledge in subjects that are totally new to us. And we'll frequently doubt whether we're doing it right.

This book aims to ease some of those problems and help you become a dedicated, determined, and agile self-learner in whatever discipline you choose. It will take you through the steps of finding your inspiration to learn, planning, developing positive habits, and driving your own education. It's my hope that you can use the skills and reasoning this book provides for any course you're interested in—and, hopefully, it will encourage you to find more subjects to learn about.

Self-learning benefits from a mindset that isn't always picked up in traditional institutions, but that can prove to be a major advantage in more than just education. That's the mindset of the *autodidact.*

An autodidact is, most simply put, a self-educator. It's what you're probably aspiring to. They own the entire method of their instruction, from beginning to finish, from interest to implementation. They're hungry to learn more about the topics they're most passionate about, and they're enthusiastic about learning new subjects from scratch. They manage all the tools they need to learn: books, videos, podcasts, online courses, and even "fieldwork." An autodidact is comfortable with the notion that they're both teacher and student, often at the same time.

Anyone can be an autodidact—there aren't any restrictions on age, gender, or background. All that's required is the willingness to actively find new knowledge and to do so with a discerning, evaluative mind. The autodidact is driven by a strong desire to acquire intelligence and is most successful when they make a concentrated and well-plotted endeavor to do so. An autodidact is especially effective if they have a strong memory and can direct their own study outside of formal education settings.

This is a skill to be cultivated. It's not easy, especially at first, but this mindset is how to take your self-learning to the next level. It's how you are able to immerse yourself in new knowledge and reach expert levels, even if you have to drag yourself through it.

Traditional Learning vs. Self-Learning

All of us have some experience in institutionalized learning, and it's important that we do. Some of us may have had good experiences in high school and college; some of us might have struggled. We all needed to go through traditional school because it laid the groundwork for our adult lives, whether we were star students or rebels.

That said, there are some elements of traditional education that could be considered impediments to true learning. These elements aren't *always* negative, and their being obstacles has a lot to do with the student. But several well-respected, learned individuals—including Mark Twain and Albert Einstein, both legendary autodidacts—have expressed skepticism about the limits of traditional education. While their criticisms aren't always true across the board, they're definitely valid in certain cases, and they're legitimate arguments in favor of self-education.

It's psychologically restrictive. In a traditional education setting, you're expected to always be attentive and on point. Most if not all of your mental resources need to be applied toward the topics you're studying, to the extent that grabbing just a few reasonable minutes of free time could make one feel guilty or irresponsible. How can you enjoy the rare two-hour movie when you've got a chemistry final breathing down your neck? This is one of the many problems with a one-size-fits-all approach.

It often uses fear as a motivator. If you don't study hard and achieve success according to the standards of your school or university, supposedly you'll have no future. Beginning when we're children, we're told that if we don't follow the demands of traditional schooling—if we don't keep our heads down for 18 years, plug away, and get that degree—then we'll wind up destitute, unsuccessful, and live a terrible life out on the fringes of society.

The problem with using fear as a motivator is that it flat-out doesn't work—we'll explain why in a bit. Sure, children might not understand motivation in many other ways, but there are indeed *other* ways.

It limits or even destroys creativity. In school, you do as you're told. You don't have any leeway. Your course of study is chosen for you. Your texts are assigned. Your materials, lab experiments, and resources all come from prepared lists from which you can't deviate. There is only one answer. Most of the time, there is only one method as well. You're told to approach problems and questions in certain, specific, and fixed manners. Even if you can better understand a concept through creative thinking and self-driven investigations, you're expected to conform. The compounding frustration, as it turns out, either turns you off the subject or doesn't teach you anything at all, usually both.

It makes you close-minded. Ivy League colleges deserve their high reputations. But let's be honest: they often create a social hierarchy based on who went through the proper channels and who deserves what. It's not just confined to highly ranked universities, of course. The culture surrounding much of traditional education tells that there is truly only one path, and that's the path they took; anyone else is illegitimate. How could someone do the same job as me when I have a bachelor of arts in sociology from a four-year university? Well... pretty easily, actually.

It actually hinders future learning. After 20 years of force-fed learning—tens of thousands of hours of lecture, reading, studying, and accumulating facts—you're almost conditioned not to learn in any other way. You don't imagine that there even *is* another way, much less that you are able to direct it yourself. You believe learning is to sit and absorb and then demonstrate said absorption.

Many are the students who've experienced so much burn-out from institutional learning that the last thing they want to do upon graduation is learn *anything.* Some students get so burned out from having their noses buried in textbooks that even the prospect of recreational reading for fun turns them off. When you've spent an entire quarter-life enduring the hardships of a strict educational setting, it can distort your view of all education going forward.

These flaws of institutionalized learning aren't universal, and they shouldn't become excuses for one to abandon their studies. But they do illustrate some of the psychological barriers a traditional education can reinforce and can explain why it can be difficult to retain the information we're supposed to learn in school. *You're told what to care about and how to think.* This just isn't a sustainable formula for engagement and knowledge retention.

In contrast, self-education carries a few potential advantages that don't necessarily arise in the scope of traditional education. They can be of great benefit—not just for your personal intelligence and self-esteem, but for "real-world" scenarios as well.

You can dive as deeply into a subject as you want. All institutionalized school courses are finite. They can't cover everything about a given subject because they're beholden to time. But in self-learning you don't have to follow a strict curriculum. There are no limits to what you can learn, and you can go much more deeply into your subject than your college professor had time for.

You go at your own pace, and you are only limited by your motivation and discipline. You can decide your own level of difficulty. With self-learning you don't have to stop and can go as far and as quickly as you want to. Or you could do the opposite: learn more deliberately at your own pace, taking all the time you need to fully understand a topic. Both scenarios are just fine.

You can set yourself up for lifelong learning. Your college degree doesn't have to be the ending point of your education, yet that's exactly how many students view it. With self-learning you can develop habits, skills, and interests that will prepare you for learning for the rest of your life by deepening your expertise in a subject and keeping up with the latest developments. Traditional education is about reading and regurgitation. Surely this is not the best approach to keep up in life, and there are other approaches that can be more beneficial.

You can study subjects with a different perspective. Most university graduates are set on a certain, limited career track. They study with a specific purpose and aim for what to do with their newfound knowledge. Even if they achieve success in their fields, these times of rapid change can make their positions less secure, since employees are expected to keep up and know more about different topics than in the past.

For example: learning solely business Japanese instead of how to use it in daily settings. Committing to self-learning gives you the upper hand because it allows you to learn with broad purposes, different purposes, or no purpose at all. This is a stark contrast to learning inside the box, oriented toward a specific perspective.

You can develop self-discipline. Charting your own course in education involves planning, personal management, commitment, and execution. When you can develop those skills yourself, they become more meaningful than when someone else tries to force them upon you. Building self-discipline is one of the handiest "by-products" of self-education because it can be replicated in all other areas of your life.

You can open up new and unique possibilities. You probably didn't have time for all the things you wanted to learn while you were in college—you were on a set course of specific study and couldn't waver too much from it. Self-learning lets you pick up all those interests and passions you might have had to set aside in formal education. You can also develop expertise in new subjects that could broaden your career potential.

Studies have shown that people, on average, have five to seven careers throughout their lifetimes. Will you be limited by your lack of self-learning abilities, or will you be able to seamlessly transition from one career to the next?

The Learning Success Pyramid

The benefits of self-learning are pretty compelling, and I'm of the firm belief that anyone can do it. But as with any endeavor in life, self-learning isn't operated by a switch that you can just flick on. It's best when there's some mental and emotional groundwork in place to prepare you for success. And of course, a helpful book such as this one never hurt anyone.

Legendary college basketball coach John Wooden was also an astute personal philosopher who developed "the pyramid of success." He intended it as a diagram to guide students through 15 different "blocks" on the course to success in their personal and practical ventures.

Wooden's model has been appropriated by several others who have sought to provide roadmaps for success or accomplishment, including educator Susan Kruger. She developed the *learning success pyramid*, which identifies the necessary elements one must bring to ensure accomplishment in learning throughout their life. Thoughtfully, Kruger kept her number of blocks to three, down from Wooden's 15:

- confidence
- self-management

- learning

Confidence. At the base of Kruger's pyramid is the self-conviction that we *can* learn. There's no way around this prerequisite, and brain chemistry has something to do with it.

When we receive information of any kind, it travels up the spinal cord toward the neural networks of the brain. The first part of the brain to get this information is the emotional center—before the analytical or interpretive parts. Predictably, this causes some problems in our daily life. The job of the emotional center is to determine if the information we get poses a threat to our security.

If this part of the brain perceives a threat, then it saps chemical resources from the rest of the brain to deal with the threat. Of course, you know this as the *fight-or-flight response*, in which our bodies are triggered into arousal to avoid bodily harm in one way or another.

The emotional center doesn't distinguish between physical threats or personal ones, which means it perceives insults, harsh criticism, and condemnation with the same level of alarm that it would with a fist, a bear attack, or an oncoming truck. It's responding to a danger to our well-being, and to do so, it hoards the chemicals we'd normally use for other brain-driven activity—such as learning.

So motivating someone to learn by threats or reproach isn't just ineffective—it's impossible. If one is feeling hurt or mistrusted, or if they're dealing with depression, stress, difficult personal issues, or fear, they don't have any resources left to help them learn.

Therefore, it's important to establish a real sense of confidence that we have the ability to learn. If you're running low in this area, be kind to yourself and take steps to affirm your learning abilities. You've learned everything in your life thus far from scratch. You may feel ignorant or that you're not good enough—and that might be true, but it's only a temporary condition.

There's not a single subject you can't understand with perseverance and the occasional stretch of hard work. Resolve yourself to not giving up. Make plans for *how* you will learn. Be forgiving of yourself if you need to take a lot of time and mark your progress as you go along.

If there is a pot of gold at the end of the rainbow, and you don't think you can follow the rainbow, it starts to feel pointless. The confidence aspect of learning is what makes it possible that you will even keep reading this book.

Self-management. The next tier in the learning success pyramid is organizing one's time, resources, tools, and communication to ensure effective learning. And once again, this process is dictated by how our brain handles incoming information.

After our emotional centers are done processing new info, the next brain part to receive the data is the front brain, or the prefrontal cortex. This is a bit like our own personal assistant: it handles motor function, memory, language, problem-solving, impulse regulation, social behavior, and a bunch of other cognitive skills. When the front brain is exhausted or depleted, we experience a weariness that prevents us from getting anything done.

This is known as ego depletion (this has been recently disproven to some degree, but it is fairly undeniable that the more you have on your plate, the more tired you will grow and the less attention and effort you will put into matters in front of you).

The best way to combat this "brain drain" is by working on self-management skills, particularly organization. This simply means taking a lot of time ahead of any task to set up systems, routines, and actions that will make the task easier to execute on an ongoing basis. Preparation is often the critical difference between success and failure, so it's vital not to rush through it. This is a skill that may have lay dormant since traditional education was all about imposing a rigorous schedule. But since we must become student and teacher simultaneously, we cannot afford to neglect this.

For the self-learner, this process means organizing yourself and your materials to facilitate gathering information, studying, comprehending, and testing yourself on what you've learned. How will you schedule your reading time? What resources will you use to track your progress and determine where your knowledge gaps are? How will you produce what you've learned—writing, video, a project, or some other means?

Think of this step as sort of a lab report. Before a scientist gets started on an experiment, they write down their hypothesis (or whatever they want to accomplish or prove) and the methods and materials they'll use to arrive at their conclusions. After each stage of their experiment, they record results and indicate what kind of adjustments they might need to make for future trials. Finally, at the end, they write out the overall results and explain what the conclusions actually mean.

Applying this mindset to self-learning, this means putting a framework in place at the beginning that details how you're going to execute. If you're teaching yourself a foreign language, you'd want to make a list of books and online audio resources you'll be using. You might want to make a list of how you'll practice and test yourself—maybe with an online sound recorder or a smartphone. And at the end of the course, maybe you'll translate a hefty amount of English text into the language you're learning.

This step might seem a little laborious, especially when you just want to jump into the material. But it will save a huge amount of time down the road and help you learn infinitely more. Regulating yourself into learning better is important because once you have led the horse to water (once you have found the resources), the horse must drink the water itself (you must do it yourself).

Learning. Well, here you are. With your confidence and self-management levels up to par, you're all set up to learn. Learning is handled by the back brain, which oversees memory, connections, recognition, vision, and meaning, among other functions. This is known as the hippocampus. It's where all the information will be processed and analyzed. It's where information is converted from short-term memory into long-term memory and where real physical structural changes in the brain will occur.

The thing is, learning itself is not a difficult task. But most people make the mistake of believing that this third stage is where they should begin, rather than addressing their confidence and self-regulation issues. Once you can overcome those hurdles in the learning pyramid, or at least address them, self-learning becomes far easier.

Arts and Sciences

The pyramid of learning success outlines the internal assets we need to have in place to embark on education, whether in institutional or self-learning. But with all the subjects we have at our disposal, are there certain courses of study that are more effective in self-education than others?

Any subject can be self-taught with proper planning and execution, whether it's playing music or learning world history or statistics. They're all possible; however, there are some topics that are indeed better suited to the act of self-education than others—and it boils down to the difference between arts and sciences.

Every subject or discipline is either an "art" or a "science"—not just the obvious ones like sculpture and biology. The difference between arts and sciences is related to the variation between subjective and objective learning and the role that teachers play in disseminating the information.

In the arts, everything is *subjective*. There are, ultimately, no right or wrong answers in art. Sure, you can be taught "proper" brush strokes or the "proper" way to calibrate a video camera. But it's not an absolute necessity to do those things in a regimented way to produce a proper piece of art. (It might be horribly difficult, but it's not impossible.) If the goal of art is to evoke an emotion, and emotion is subjective, then there are innumerable paths to achieve that goal.

The content of a course in the arts is changeable, and a huge part of it depends on the instructor. They have their own interpretations of the material they're teaching, and it could be entirely different from a teacher in the same subject in another school. There are no ironclad "facts" in the arts, and because of that the teacher is indivisible from the subject they're teaching. Without strong reference points and milestones, this is harder in self-learning.

Science, on the other hand, is *objective.* You deal exclusively with proven facts and hard data. The speed of light, the physical makeup of elements on the periodic table, and the product of 2 × 4 are inarguable. You can't really have an *opinion* about whether or not the answers are true; they are whether you like it or not. You can learn formulas and how to apply them—they will never change or let you down.

Likewise, every science or math teacher in the world has to tell you these facts. It doesn't matter *how* they teach them to you or how they interpret or feel about them. They all have to teach you the same concepts, because it's literal and true. If a math teacher is telling you 2 × 4 = 13, they're not going to be teaching too much longer. So objective sciences don't rely on the presence of a certain type of teacher—whether they're there or not, the facts are still going to be the facts. This is more reliable and dependable to learn on your own as compared to the arts.

In self-learning, though, *you're* your own instructor. The only personality you have to deal with is your own. You might read the opinions and interpretations of other people, but the final funnel is your own brain. You're tasked with seeking out relevant material and instilling it in your own head.

Because of this, there's at least a little credence to the idea that sciences are more suitable for self-education than the arts. No matter what branch of science you study—

physical science, law, statistics, or economics—there will be a hard set of indisputable data that you'll have to accept at some point. Those concrete truths are easier to establish than the more flexible theories of the arts. So as a self-learner, the objective course of science study may be more suitable.

This does not mean it's impossible to teach yourself an artistic subject. I've spent a lot of time on my own working on my writing skills, for example, and don't see myself stopping anytime soon. Teaching yourself an art is entirely possible. You just need to make certain small adjustments in your approach to the subject.

Self-Motivation

The rewards of self-learning are instantaneously obvious, but make no mistake: it's an ambitious effort. You're serving as both student and teacher. It requires confidence, commitment, and good planning. If you're not a traditional "self-starter," the goal may look so work-heavy

31

that it might seem hard to work up the motivation to plow through to it.

Self-learning isn't like typical school, where someone or something else is responsible for setting your goals and motivating you to work toward them. It's also different from work, where your motivation is simple: finish your job and get paid. Besides, this "carrot-and-stick" motivation strategy doesn't always result in you producing your best work, and even if you get the requisite compensation for completing your work successfully, there's a great chance you won't derive a lot of satisfaction from it.

We call that reward-or-punishment framework *extrinsic motivation*: the compensation you get comes from an external source, such as the company you work for or the school district you study in. Somebody else is generating your payments or rewards according to guidelines that they set up—not you. This kind of motivation might have worked for a while in the past, when options for study and employment were more limited and people just wanted to survive.

The opposite of this concept is *intrinsic motivation*. Rather than performing a task to gain rewards or avoid punishment from someone else, a person experiencing intrinsic motivation does an activity for how it will enrich them on an intangible level. The rewards one gets in this framework are self-generated: pride, sense of accomplishment, enjoyment, rising to a challenge. These kinds of rewards, quite simply, *feel* better and have more personal meaning than a paycheck or a grade.

Research over the last fifty years or so has consistently found that intrinsic rewards are far more motivating than extrinsic ones. In fact, studies conducted in the 1970s by professors Harry Harlow and Edward Deci found that extrinsic motivation actually *detracts* from intrinsic motivation: if you're doing a job because you both get money and seek personal satisfaction from it, the motive for outside rewards will diminish the quality of the internal rewards you pursue.

Author Daniel Pink has written several key works on his theories of contemporary motivation. In current times, he says, the idea of "Motivation 3.0" is more likely to bring about the personal success we all desire. This follows the eras of Motivation 1.0, which is merely the primitive need to survive, and Motivation 2.0, the reward-and-punishment model your parents might have experienced in theirs.

Motivation 3.0 is all about intrinsic motivation. It's spurred by Pink's belief that "the secret to high performance isn't our biological drive or our reward-and-punishment drive, but our third drive—our deep-seated desire to direct our own lives, to extend and expand our abilities, and to make a contribution." Pink described three different factors that make up intrinsic motivation.

Autonomy. Freedom is a big, driving impulse for everyone. Having autonomy means that you are completely in control of your own life. You're behind the steering wheel, you're making the decisions, and you're generating your own rewards. You're not answering to the demands of anybody else and you're able to set your own agenda.

Autonomy motivates us because we want to believe that only we truly affect our own lives. Nobody actually enjoys the prospect of somebody else manipulating the levers in their existence; it implies that we're being restricted by somebody else's expectations or wishes. We're bred to want independence because it increases our own reserves of self-worth and personal power.

In motivation for self-learning, you might use the factor of autonomy to envision how your life might improve after you gain your knowledge. For example, you might be motivated to teach yourself coding because you can picture yourself running your own web design contract business in the future. You might learn a language because you want to spend some time living in a foreign country. Or you just want to learn cooking because you're tired of making macaroni and cheese from a box using ingredients someone else chose. The point is that it's your choice alone.

Mastery. There's nothing like the satisfaction of knowing you're doing something well, that you've worked and practiced hard to achieve your own standards of excellence. That's what mastery is: the drive to improve our skills or knowledge in areas we're passionate about.

Mastery is a motivating factor because it gives us a sense of progress (at least if we can stick it out through the beginning phases of learning something brand new, when we're bound to be frustrated from time to time). We keep pushing through in areas because we want to learn something new every day. We want to arrive at a point where we do only what we want to do, without being sidetracked or stunted by "busy work" or purposeless tasks. We want a sense of accomplishment that we can draw upon daily.

Mastery might be the most obvious stimulating component in self-learning. You might be driven to understand every nuance of Shakespeare's work, build a mechanical go-cart from scratch, become an ace audio producer, or understand all the ins and outs of business contracts without having to call a lawyer. The goal of every student is to gain expertise in their field, and a great self-learner keeps the prospect of mastery uppermost in their mind at all points in their journey. Mastery is doubly gratifying when you know that it's because of you and your drive alone, rather than following the droning of a set of professors.

Purpose. Although part of the definition of intrinsic motivation is doing something for its own sake, there's also merit in the belief that we're doing something for the "greater good." That's what a sense of purpose delivers. We believe that what we're doing has a positive effect on more than just our personal lives—it's also contributing to the general goodwill of the planet, helping somebody other than ourselves, or restoring a sense of higher meaning in our lives.

We're driven by purpose because, well, deep down inside, none of us really want to be jerks. We want to believe that we're "good" people, that we're responding to the highest calls of nature and society. We want to believe that we offer something important to the world, that our efforts are making others' existences more valuable, satisfied, or simply happy. This doesn't necessarily conflict with our desires for autonomy—yes, we crave independence and self-direction, but we also want to believe we're worthy members of the human race as well.

A self-learner might want to study philosophy because they seek a more enlightened state of mind. They'll teach themselves about agriculture because they want to contribute to a community organic garden. Perhaps someone studies political science because they want to understand and spur changes in local government. Or they'll teach themselves clowning because they enjoy making children happy (given that they're not one of those "scary" clowns).

During the course of self-learning, it will always help to orient your mind toward the internal rewards and improvements you're seeking. Inspiration is, invariably, a stronger force than compulsion. Keeping your eye on what you will give *yourself* through self-learning will always be a strong, guiding force in your studies, and nobody can provide that to you but yourself.

Takeaways:

- Self-learning is a pursuit that isn't new, but what's new is how possible and attainable it is. The world is your oyster, courtesy of the Internet, and we have the ability to learn anything we want these days. Traditional learning has some positive aspects, but it also severely limits our approach toward education and how we seek to enrich ourselves. To combat this, we must first take a cue from autodidacts and understand the difference in mindset between reading and regurgitation and intellectual curiosity.

- The learning success pyramid accurately lays out the three aspects of learning, two of which are typically neglected and thus serve as enormous barriers for most people. First, you must have confidence in your ability to learn, otherwise you will grow discouraged and hopeless. Second, you must be able to self-regulate your impulses, be disciplined, and focus when it matters—you can lead a horse to water, but you can't make him drink. Third comes learning, which is where most people tend to start—to their detriment. Learning is more than picking up a book and reading, at least psychologically.

- Self-motivation is related to self-regulation. It's an essential aspect of self-learning because there is no educator to impose rigidity upon you—just yourself. You are both the teacher and the student, and that comes with the task of self-motivation. There are three main aspects of intrinsic motivation to keep yourself moving toward your goal of self-learning: autonomy, mastery, and purpose/impact. The intangibles tend to be far more powerful than what you would traditionally consider motivating.

Chapter 2. Interaction with Information

Jorge is fascinated with archaeology—from a distance, that is. He's been interested in it ever since he saw *Raiders of the Lost Ark*. So he's decided to try and teach himself about it by picking up as many books as he can— five, to be exact. All at the same time. He downloads them on his e-reader.

For a couple of days, these five books don't do much except look back at him through his screen. He didn't think through which of the books would be most suitable for his expertise level, which right now could charitably be described as modest. He just went for a couple that were best sellers and another because it was just $1.99. But so what? Those five books should at least be enough to familiarize him with basic archaeology knowledge. They should be catered to people that are starting from ground zero. He should be able to pick up what he needed. *Should, should, should*—the bane of all reasonable expectations.

Jorge starts to read one of the books, by an archaeologist who had extensive experience working at the pyramids in Egypt. He figures that he should start with someone that was right at the source, not taking into consideration his own level of expertise. This book has a long preface, but he never reads prefaces. He just wants to get to the meat.

The first chapter instantly gives him a roadblock. There are a bunch of long words that seem specific to archaeologists that he doesn't get. But that's okay—he'll just power through it because he's a fast reader. He read all the volumes of the *Hunger Games* series in a week. He'll get this, no problem.

Jorge is mentally depleted at the end of the first chapter because he hasn't considered anything he's read. He doesn't know what it means or why it's important. He had to keep reading paragraphs over and over, though he stubbornly refused to consult a dictionary. He still finished Chapter 1 relatively quickly, but he has no interest in moving on to Chapter 2. It's too depressing and discouraging. So he picks up another book that he got and has the exact same experience.

Jorge considers this all a divine sign and decides he wasn't meant to study archaeology at all. He thinks he clearly doesn't have the mental resources necessary to pursue the subject. So he closes his e-book, a little depressed and dejected, thinking that he's too stupid.

But Jorge isn't stupid. In fact, he was one of the best students in his high school class, and he routinely aced tests without studying. His downfall was his expectations of his own initial abilities and how they would react to new knowledge and reading material. He might be smart, but not in *this* field. When he failed to immediately grasp it, he considered it his own personal failure. But that's only because he tried to read a book of knowledge the same way that he read juvenile fiction—or anything that was thrown at him in high school. He had no plan and wasn't prepared for what self-learning really requires.

Since those styles of writing are completely different, and because you also have a different purpose in mind (assimilation and comprehension of new information and knowledge), they need to be *approached* in completely different ways. Interacting with information isn't just about expectations— it's about planning. To start with, Jorge should have tried using the SQ3R method— a method that can be transformative in your self-learning quest.

The SQ3R Method

For the large majority of school subjects, textbooks are the core of the study program along with lectures and discussions. A typical teacher's entire lesson plan for a year usually draws from the structure and sequence of at least one textbook. These volumes are, more often than not, forbiddingly big. Multiply one large book by the number of classes a student has in any given semester and you've got a seriously overweight backpack—nearly as heavy as every one of your teachers' expectations that you read every single one.

Textbooks are dense, detailed, heavily annotated, and long. It's easy to conjure up the image of a student late at night, glossing over page 349 of a giant volume, growing fatigued and unable to retain the words they're reading the next morning.

That's why American educator Francis P. Robinson developed a method meant to help students really get the most comprehension from the texts they're assigned—and, ergo, the subject they're studying. Robinson sought a way to make reading more active, helping readers by creating dynamic engagement with books so the information stuck in their minds.

The traditional classroom setting of reading and regurgitating certainly isn't the most effective, but it's the only model most of us know. Robinson's approach is suitable for more than just reading: your entire study plan can be modeled on Robinson's method and adapted to your self-learning.

The technique is called The SQ3R method, named for its five components:

- survey

- question

- read

- recite

- review

Survey. The first step in the method is getting a general overview of what you'll be reading. Textbooks and nonfiction works aren't like fiction or narrative literature in which you just start from the beginning and wind your way through each chapter. The best works of nonfiction are arranged to impart information in a way that's clear and memorable and builds upon each previous chapter. If you go dive in without surveying first, you are going in blind, without understanding where you are going and what you are trying to accomplish. You should get a lay of the land first, *before* you delve into Chapter 1. The survey component is for you to get the most general introduction to the topic so you can establish and shape the goals you want to achieve from reading the book.

It's just like taking a look at the entire map before you set off on a road trip. You may not need all the knowledge at the moment, but understanding everything as a whole and how it fits together will help you with the small details and when you're in the weeds. You'll know that you generally need to head southwest if you're confused.

In the SQ3R method, surveying means examining the structure of the work: the book title, the introduction or preface, section titles, chapter titles, headings and subheadings. If the book is illustrated with pictures or graphics, you'd review them. You could also make note of the conventions the book uses to guide your reading: typefaces, bold or italic text, and chapter objectives and study questions if they're in there. In using the survey step, you're setting up expectations for what you're going to be reading about and giving yourself an initial framework to structure your goals for reading the material.

For example, let's say you're reading a book to learn more about geology. I happen to have one called *Geology Illustrated* by John S. Shelton—it's about 50 years old and no longer in print, but it works fine for our purposes.

There's a preface describing what's in the book and how the illustrations are arranged. There's an unusually extensive table of contents, divided into parts: "Materials," "Structure," "Sculpture," "Time," "Case Histories," and "Implications." That tells me that the book will start with concrete (excuse the pun) geological elements, will flow into how they form over time, important incidents, and what we might expect in the future. That's a pretty good guess at the arc of the book.

Each part is then divided into chapters, which are further divided into a ton of headings and subheadings—too many to mention here, but they give a more nuanced summary of what each part will go into. When you survey and know the significance of what you're currently learning, you are able to instantly comprehend it better. It's the difference between looking at a single gear in isolation versus seeing where and how it works in a complex clock.

Beyond books, you should survey all the important concepts in a discipline. If you can't find it within a structure like a book's table of contents, then you need to be able to create it for yourself. Yes, this is the difficult part, but once you are able to lay all the concepts out and understand how they relate to each other at least on a surface level, you will already be leaps ahead of others. Use the survey component to form an outline of what you'll learn. In a sense, it's more like you're plotting out a metaphorical "book" for yourself.

You want to form a general outline of what you're going to learn. Since you're studying this on your own, there might be a few gaps in what you think you'll need to know. So in this phase, you'll want to determine exactly what you *want* to become knowledgeable about, as specifically as you can make it. For example, if you want to learn all about psychology, that's going to take a significant amount of time. It won't happen in one shot. You'd want to specify it a little more: the early history of psychoanalysis, the works of Sigmund Freud and Carl Jung, sports psychology, developmental psychology—the possibilities are plenty.

You'll want to keep an eye out for phrases or concepts that appear in several different sources, since they represent elements that come up often in your chosen field and might be things you have to know. Draw connections and cause-and-effect relationships before even diving into any of the concepts in detail.

For example, let's say you want to study the history of European cinema. Entering "European cinema history" into Google brings up a lot of interesting possibilities, and some of those can be used to form the outline you want.

You can look for reading materials on Amazon.com, finding the ones that seem the most authoritative. The Internet Movie Database (IMDB) can help you find the most important European films for you to watch. You can discover which European directors are the most cited and appear to be the most important and influential. You can research which European movies are the highest rated and why. You can collect a few resources on what specific countries had what cinematic movements and why.

Then you'll organize these resources. You'll come up with a plan to study each one—perhaps study a chapter in a book on early European film history, then watch a couple of films that represent the era you're on at the moment and give yourself a film review assignment afterward. Focus on gathering and organizing; you don't need to touch them yet. The important aspect is that you've surveyed the topic before diving in and thus understand what you're getting into and why.

Question. In the second stage of the SQ3R method, you're still not diving into the deep end. During the question stage, you'll work a little more deeply to get your mind more prepared to focus and interact with the material you're reading. You'll take a slightly closer look at the structure of the book and form some questions you wanted answered or set up the objectives you want to achieve.

In the question phase of reading a book— or, more precisely at this point, *preparing* to read—you'd go through the chapter titles, headings, and subheadings are rephrase them in the form of a question. This turns the dry title the author has given into a challenge or problem for you to solve. For example, if you're reading a book on Freud, there might be a chapter called "Foundations of Freud's Analyses of Dreams." You'd rewrite this chapter title as "How did Sigmund Freud's work on dream interpretation originate and what were his very first ideas on the subject?" You could pencil that question in the margin of your book. If you're reading a textbook with study questions at the ends of the chapters, those serve as excellent guides to what you're about to find out.

In the geology book, I'm afraid there aren't too many chapter titles that I could rephrase as inquiries. ("Weathering," "Groundwater," "Glaciation"—that's about it.) But there are headings that might work: "Some Effects of Metamorphism on Sedimentary Rocks," for example, can become "What can happen to bottom-centered rocks through eons of environmental change?" Not only have I changed it to a question, but I've paraphrased the title into wording that I can understand even before I've started reading.

Now that you've organized your resources for study planning, you can arrange some of the topics you're going to cover into questions you want answered or objectives that you want to meet. Based on the source material you've lined up and the patterns that you might have observed, what specific answers are you hoping to find in your studies? Write them down. This is also a good time to come up with a structure for answering your questions—a daily journal, a self-administered quiz, some kind of "knowledge tracker"? You don't have to answer the questions yet—you just need to know how you're going to record them when you do.

In our European film history example, if you've done even the most cursory investigation in the survey phase, you undoubtedly came across some directors' names more than once: Federico Fellini, Jean-Luc Godard, Luis Buñuel, Fritz Lang, and so forth. You figure they're going to be important people to get to know, so you could ask the question, "Why was Fellini so influential?" "What was Buñuel's directing style?" "What themes did Godard pursue in his filmmaking?" You might have come across certain concepts or themes that seemed common in European film—"French New Wave," "World War II," "neorealism," for example. Put these down as targets for your study and arrange them into your outline.

Reading. In this stage you're finally ready to dive into the material. Because you've gotten the lay of the land and formed some questions and goals for your studies, you're a little more engaged when you finally sit down to read. You're looking for answers to the questions you've raised. Another underrated aspect of formulating and organizing before you actually begin reading is to build *anticipation* for learning. You've been looking over everything for a while now, and you'll probably be eager to finally dive in and answer the questions you've been mentally accumulating.

This step is where most people try to start but fail because they lack a foundation and instead have unreasonable expectations.

Now you're being deliberate and paced about your reading so you can comprehend better. This means slowing down—a *lot.* Be patient with the material and with yourself. If a passage is difficult to understand, read it extremely slowly. If you aren't getting a sense of clarity about a certain part, stop, go back to the beginning, and reread it. It's not like you're reading a page-turner novel that you can't put down. You're reading information that might be densely packed— so read it slowly and attentively, one section at a time.

Chances are that reading is part of your study plan, but so might visual aids, online courses, and Internet resources. Use them exactly the way you'd use the book in the reading phase: deliberately and persistently, with the goal of fully understanding each concept you're being taught. If you get lost, remember the rewind button and scrolling are your best buddies. Plan your study time around getting as complete a level of comprehensiveness as you can.

With our European film history example, this is obvious. Watch your films with a critical eye. At certain points you might want to rewind to catch visual images, dialogue, or action that might be pertinent. If you can watch a video with a director's commentary audio track, you'll want to spend an afternoon with that. Cross-check the movies with the books you're reading or the online courses you're taking to answer any questions or lines of thought that you might have.

Reciting. This step is crucial in processing the information you're learning about and is the biggest difference between reading to learn and reading for entertainment. Now that you're familiar with the material, the aim of the reciting phase is to reorient your mind and attention to focus and learn more fully as you go along. In other words, this step is about literal recitation.

Ask questions—out loud, verbally—about what you're reading. This is also the point where you take copious notes in the margins of the text and underline or highlight key points. Recitation is verbal and also through writing. However, it's important to restate these points *in your own words* rather than just copy phrases from the book onto a piece of paper. By doing this, you're taking the new knowledge and putting it into phrases of which you already know the meaning. This makes the information easier to grasp in a language you understand. It makes it significant and meaningful to you.

My geology book happens to have pretty wide margins on the sides of the pages, so I have some nice room to rephrase and rewrite key points as well as highlight important concepts. For example, consider the following original text:

> "This comparison suggests that the slow progress of erosion on hills and mountains is similar to the much more rapid and observable changes seen in miniature all about us."

I could rewrite the above into something like this:

> "Mountains and hills experience the same decay as happens in lowlands and rivers, just more slowly. Similar to baseball players."

What I'm doing here is putting one single bit of information into two distinct phrases, one of which I had to come up with myself. This is a huge tool that's used in memorization, and it's also a great way to make the information more meaningful to me personally. I also added a bit about baseball because I like baseball, and it makes the concept instantly understandable when I look back at it. Repeated throughout the course of a whole book, this process multiplies your learning capacity by itself.

The recitation phase in organizing your studies is great because it works across different mediums, and there are plenty of ways you can express your questions and restatements.

Going back to our European cinema example, if you're watching Ingmar Bergman's *The Seventh Seal* (short summary: medieval knight meets angel of death, tries to buy time by playing chess with him), you might write down questions about its Biblical references, the art direction, the Middle Ages references, or the cinematography. You could also write a summary or do a video blog of the movie and address the key sequences that are most relevant to your questions. You could also compare it to other films by Bergman or note similarities his style has with other directors that you're studying. The important part is that you are taking the time to rephrase and recite new knowledge and make it meaningful to you—and no one else.

Review. The final stage of the SQ3R plan is when you go back over the material that you've studied, re-familiarize yourself with the most important points, and build your skills at memorizing the material.

Robinson breaks this stage down into specific days of the week, but we'll just mention some of the tactics in general. They include writing more questions of important parts you have highlighted, orally answering some of the questions if you can, reviewing your notes, creating flashcards for important concepts and terminology, rewriting the table of contents using your own words, and building out a mind map. Any kind of practice that helps you drill down, take in, and commit information to memory is fair game (though flashcards are especially effective).

This step is meant to strengthen your memory of the material, but it does more than that. It can help you see connections and similarities between different aspects that you might not have picked up at first and put concepts and ideas into greater context. It can also improve your mental organization skills so you can use this practice for other topics.

Think of this step as the natural continuation of the survey step. At this point, you've gained an outline of the field, you've gotten into the nitty-gritty, and now you should take a step back, reevaluate, and make updated, more accurate, and insightful connections. Pair that with memorization, and your path to self-learning and expertise becomes essentially a shortcut.

My geology book has no shortage of terms that I could put onto flashcards. "Monocline," "stratification," "glacial scour"—whip out the Sharpie now. But I could also map out the process of glaciation in a flowchart or some other visual medium. I could make a timeline of the ages of the earth and link it with the most significant geological changes that took place during each era. I can also take down questions that come up that the book either left unanswered or made me want to investigate more fully.

You can use most elements of the book review phase for study planning in the same way. In our European cinema example, you could make a catalog or database for European film directors that outlines their work, their main themes, or their stylistic choices. You can draw up flashcards that will help you recall the important facets of different European strains: "neo-realism," "giallo horror," "spaghetti Western," and "cinéma du look." And of course you can journal what you've learned, either in written form or some visual expression.

The SQ3R method is no joke. It's exhaustive and detailed and will take patience and sharp organization to pull off. But if you give yourself the patience and devotion to take each step seriously and slowly, you'll find it incredibly helpful to tackle a complex subject. And each time you do it, it's a little easier than the last.

In explaining the SQ3R method, we briefly skimmed the role of organization and notes and how they impact self-learning. After all, you can't organize everything in your head only and hope to be effective. When you eventually need to write down what you've learned or organized, there is a specific method of note-taking that will be most beneficial.

Cornell Notes

The most famous method of note-taking is called the *Cornell method*, and elements relate to what we covered earlier. Here's how it works.

On a handwritten sheet for note-taking (writing by hand is key), split it down the middle and into two columns. Make the column on the right about twice the size as the column on the left. Label the right column "Notes" and label the left column "Cues." Leave a couple inches empty at the bottom of the page and label that section "Summary."

You now have three distinct sections, but you will only be taking notes in the Notes section on the right. This is where you take normal notes on the bigger concepts with supporting detail as concisely as possible.

Write everything you need to make a thorough assessment of what you're learning. Make sure to skip some space between points so you can fill in more detail and clarification at a later point. Draw charts and diagrams, make lists where appropriate, and give your best effort to capturing what matters.

You don't need to think about organization or highlighting while you are taking the initial notes. Just write what you hear or read and give as complete of a picture as possible. Record as much as possible in the right column, as you just want to capture information at this point. Don't discriminate. When you go over the notes again, you can figure out what is necessary and important.

After you're done taking notes, move on to the left Cues side. This is where, for each section or concept, you filter and analyze the Notes side and write the important parts on the Cues side. Where the Notes side is more of a jumbled mess, the Cues side is a relatively organized account of the topic at hand—basically, the same information is on each side.

Turn five sentences of normal notes into one or two sentences with a main point and supporting facts. Hopefully you can picture it: on the left is an organized set of statements that sum everything up neatly, while on the right is a jumble of messy writing. At this point, you've already achieved the second level of taking notes as we talked about before. You've already gone a level above what you normally do, and you can already skim the paper and instantly know what the notes are about.

Finally, after you're done with the Notes and Cues sides, move to the Summary section at the bottom.

This is where you attempt to summarize everything you've just taken notes on into a few top-level ideas and statements, with only the important supporting facts or exceptions to the rules. You want to say as much in as few words as possible because, when you review your notes, you want to be able to understand quickly and not have to deconstruct and analyze all over again.

You want to be able to skim the Summary and Cues section and move on. Where you previously had one page full of messy notes, now you have a short Summary section where you can instantly gain understanding of new information. It also allows you to memorize more effectively, as again it's just a few sentences versus a page you would have to analyze every time. And once again, synthesizing for one more repetition doesn't hurt.

As a quick example, why we don't we review what we've been talking about in this lesson? Suppose we are taking Cornell notes on this concept itself. On the right side will be as much as you can capture. It won't be verbatim, and you'll probably need to write in short phrases.

But it is not too organized—it's just a mass of information based on what you've heard. On the left side, you'll have a few shorter phrases, such as the four stages of notes and what happens in each stage, how Cornell notes function, and their importance in learning better.

As for the Summary section—you would boil everything you've learned from this lesson down into one or two sentences—there are four stages of learning: taking notes, editing, analysis, reflection. Cornell notes force you to go through all four stages and help you organize information better with three sections to enforce information.

You have created your own study guide. Better yet, you also have the entire process you used to create it documented on the same page, from original notes to synthesis and summarization. You have a record of information that allows you to go as deep as you want or refer to whatever you want. The most important part is that you've created something that has personal significance to you because you've phrased everything in a way in which you derive meaning. You are making the information fit your mental scheme, not the other way around.

Overall, taking notes is not a lazy, passive activity. That's the real secret of great notes. They are intended to serve as something you can refer to, instantly understand, and find helpful, as opposed to having to decipher them. This won't work if you have to first try to understand someone else's sense of structure and organization.

Peter Brown, author of the book *Make It Stick*, simplifies this point on notes: he maintains that when no effort is put into the learning process, it doesn't last very long.

In one study Brown cited, students were allowed to copy notes word for word on some material but were asked to rephrase *other* material in their own words. When these students were tested later, they did a far better job of recalling the material they had paraphrased themselves.

It may be convenient—for the students, if not the professor—to provide written notes for lectures. But the lack of effort this arrangement inherently has will handicap the student. In fact, the less effort and involvement a student is able to use to get by, the worse the learning will be.

Your notes are how your brain will process, understand, and memorize information. That means you need to make sure you have a good foundation to start with.

The final best practice on interacting with information for self-learners is the art of self-explanation. Again, you may recognize elements of this from the SQ3R method, specifically the part about *recitation*.

Self-Explanation

Self-explanation sounds simple, but there is a method to the simplicity. It's more than thinking out loud. It involves explaining and articulating information to establish a baseline of knowledge and blind spots.

Blind spots are when we don't realize what we don't know. But with self-explanation, you will quickly learn what you don't understand, and it might be far more than you expected. Here's how it can sometimes show itself in real life.

If you've been around small children under age seven or so, you may have witnessed (or experienced, if you're a parent) a phenomenon we call "the why chain." This is when kids ask an initial question about the world—say, "Where does rain come from?"—and, after hearing our answer ("From clouds"), continue down a path of relentless questions to get at a definitive, ending answer ("Why don't the clouds hold in the rain?" "Why can't the clouds just fall to the earth still shaped like clouds?" "Why don't the clouds on a sunny day let rain go?").

Yes, this line of questioning can be a recipe for tedium. But it's reflective of a child's innate capacity for endless curiosity for a definitive answer. (For parents, of course, this point usually comes a lot earlier.)

Elaborative interrogation has something in common with that childlike inquiry, except it relates to more advanced topics that adults are (hopefully) liable to investigate. Simply put, elaborative interrogation is an effort to create explanations for *why* stated facts are true. This is what drives home comprehension, as well as what you *don't* comprehend.

In elaborative interrogation, the learner inquires about how and why certain concepts work. Nothing is safe from this inquiry. They go through their study materials to determine the answers and try to find connections between all the ideas they're learning about. Can you answer simple questions or at least understand what the answer is likely to be?

"Why" questions are more significant than "what" questions, which primarily relate to the natures of identification and memorization. A line of "why" questions elicits a better understanding of the factors and reasons for a given subject. We can memorize all the parts of a flower—the petal, the stamen, the pistil, the receptacle, and so on—but the names alone mean nothing to us. We have to ask what each part of a flower does and why that role is integral to its lifespan.

This method is effective because it's simple and anyone can apply it easily. Elaborative interrogation does, however, require some existing knowledge about the topic to generate solid questions for yourself.

Elaborative interrogation could proceed like this, and suppose you are learning about the Great Depression of the 1930s:

- The first thing you'd ask would be, well, **what was it?** It was the biggest worldwide economic breakdown in the history of the industrialized world.

- **What caused the Great Depression?** A few key events, like the stock market crash of October 1929, the failure of over 9,000 banks, declines in consumer spending, high tax on imports from Europe, and drought conditions in the agricultural sector.

- Let's talk about the stock market crash. **Why did it happen?** Some experts were concerned about margin-selling, declines in the British stock market, out-of-control speculation, and some questionable business practices in the steel industry.

- ***Margin-selling? What was that? How did margin-selling work, and why was it a problem?*** Margin-selling (or margin-trading) is when an investor borrows money from a broker to buy stock. So many investors used it that most stock purchases were bought with this borrowed money. It worked so well that the stock prices went up—and when the asset bubble popped, prices fell off. Since the investor had no funds to repay the loan, both the broker and the investor had no profit to show for it.

And the chain of interrogation goes on from there. You use your study materials to obtain the answers to the "why" and "how" questions. Once you've sufficiently established those answers, you go back to the other aspects of the Great Depression and the stock market crash and determine how each aspect related to one another. *How did margin-selling affect the banks? How did margin-selling relate to the decline in consumer spending? Did the drought affect the trade issues with Europe?*

The overall point of elaborative interrogation is to make sure there are no holes in your understanding. If you can survive your own questioning, it's likely you can survive tests, exams, and when other people ask you to teach them. You can start with the journalistic questions (who, what, where, when, why, how), then move on to contextual questions (how did this happen and what happens after) for a good, thorough start to understanding.

The range of topics for which you can use elaborative interrogation is practically limitless. For example, math students can use it to break down advanced calculations and establish patterns that might help in higher-level math topics. If you're studying human biology, you can use the technique to determine the specific conditions that lead to medical conditions like high cholesterol or heart arrhythmia. Even students of literature can use the technique to study motifs, trends, and themes in a particular author's work.

Elaborative interrogation, when you think about it, is a form of self-explanation. You are quizzing yourself and then putting yourself on the spot as to whether you can answer or not. You should be able to see how this lets you know where you lack comprehension and facts. Having knowledge is of course important to learning, but sometimes not having blind spots is just as important.

The Feynman Technique

Elaborative interrogation is one method of asking yourself questions that focuses on you seeing the whole picture behind a piece of information. You can use the journalistic questions or contextual and background questions.

The Feynman technique, named for Nobel-prize winning physicist Richard Feynman, is another type of discussing with yourself. Known as the "Great Explainer," Feynman was revered for his ability to clearly illustrate dense topics like quantum physics for virtually anybody. In *Feynman's Lost Lecture: The Motion of Planets Around the Sun*, David Goodstein writes that Feynman prided himself on being able to explain the most complex ideas in the simplest terms. It stemmed from his own study techniques as a student at Princeton University, and he refined the method as a professor and teacher of physics.

Most of us have internal monologues in some form or another throughout most of the day. Verbalizing these conversations in the context of problem-solving spurs more cognizant attention to how your mind works through a problem.

Properly carried out, the Feynman technique will prove whether you really understand a topic or have glossed over certain important concepts. It's also suitable for almost every conceivable subject, allowing you to see the gaps in your knowledge that need to be connected.

If you feel your explanations are long, rambling, or protracted, you may not have grasped the subject as well as you may have thought.

The usefulness of the Feynman technique is especially helpful in scientific or technological topics, but it's adaptable for any subject. Literature students can use it to narrow down themes, historians can use it to explain events and historical patterns, and civics students can use it to understand living conditions or urban issues—there's really no restriction on how you can use it. All you need to do is honestly answer the questions you are asking yourself, and you will quickly see where you need to focus your attention.

The Feynman technique is a specific application of elaborative interrogation. Remember, the goal is not to actually answer the questions; it's to see what you are *unable* to answer—that is the information it provides. It has four steps.

Step one: Choose your concept.

The Feynman technique is very widely applicable, so let's choose one we can use throughout this section: gravity. Suppose that we want to either understand the basics about gravity or explain it to someone else. This can obviously differ depending on what you are learning at the moment.

Step two: Write down an explanation of the concept in plain English.

Can you do it? Is this easy or difficult? This is the truly important step because it will show exactly what you do and do not understand about the concept of gravity. Explain it as simply, yet accurately, as you can in a way that someone who knows nothing about the concept would also understand.

So going back to the concept we are using, how would *you* define gravity? Would it be something about being attracted to large masses? Would it be something that makes us fall? Or would it be about how our planet was formed? Can you do it, or will you resort to saying, "Well, you know... it's gravity!"

This step allows you to see your blind spots and where your explanation starts to fall apart. If you can't perform this step, clearly you don't know as much about it as you thought, and you would be terrible at explaining it to someone else.

You might be able to explain what happens to objects that are subject to gravity and what happens when there is zero gravity. You might also be able to explain the causes of gravity. But everything that happens in between might be something you assume you know but continually skip learning about.

Step three: Find your blind spots.

If you were unable to come up with a short description of gravity in the previous step, then it's clear you have large gaps in your knowledge. Research gravity and find a way to describe it in a simple way. You might come up with something like "The force that causes larger objects to attract smaller objects because of their weight and mass." Whatever you are unable to explain, this is a blind spot you must rectify.

Being able to analyze information and break it down in a simple way demonstrates knowledge and understanding. If you can't summarize it in one sentence, or at least in a brief and concise manner, you still have blind spots you need to learn about. This technique is how you can find them easily, and make sure you understand the concepts you are taking notes on and learning. I encourage you to take a second and try this right now. What seemingly simple concept can you try to explain? Can you actually do it, or does it reveal a lack of understanding somewhere in the process?

Step four: Use an analogy.

Finally, create an analogy for the concept. What is the purpose of this step? It's an extension of step three. Making analogies between concepts requires an understanding of the main traits and characteristics of each. This step is to demonstrate whether or not you truly understand it on a deeper level and to make it easier to explain. You can look at it as the true test of your understanding and whether you still possess blind spots in your knowledge.

For example, gravity is like when you put your foot into a pool and the fallen leaves on the surface are attracted to it because it causes a barely seen impact. That impact is gravity.

This step also connects new information to old information and lets you piggyback off a working mental model to understand or explain in greater depth. Of course, it's unlikely that you can do step four if you can't do steps two and three, but sometimes you can do steps two and three and find you can't do step four—now you understand the boundaries of your knowledge and better.

The Feynman technique is a rapid way to discover what you know versus what you think you know, and it allows you to solidify your knowledge base. When you keep explaining and simplifying to yourself and discover that you can't, you've just discovered that you don't know as much as you thought you did.

Remember, it's another extension of elaborative interrogation, which is where you quiz yourself by asking questions where you can demonstrate your comprehension or lack thereof.

Takeaways:

- Interaction with information—in other words, how to take something that's on the page and screen, understand it, and make it usable to yourself at a later time. That's learning in a nutshell, but there are best practices you should embrace outside of the traditional classroom setting.
- First is the SQ3R method. Use it. It stands for survey, question, read, recite, review. This is not just a process for attacking a book, but rather a plan for attacking entire disciplines and fields—and whatever you are trying to learn for yourself. Most people will use some elements of the SQ3R method, such as the read and review portion, but without the other elements, deeper

comprehension is rarer and more difficult.

- Second is Cornell notes. Use them. Cornell notes split your note-taking into three parts: taking notes, writing cues, and summarizing. In this way, you create your own study guide, with the ability to go into as much detail as you want on command. The fact that you've gone through the information three times also doesn't hurt.

- Finally, self-explanation. Do it. When we are forced to try to explain concepts through self-inquiry, we will quickly discover what we do know and what we don't know at all. These are called blind spots, and they are far more common than you might like to think. Can you explain why the sky is blue or how gravity works? Probably not off the top of your head, even though you think you understand those concepts. The Feynman technique is an offshoot of self-explanation that helps find blind spots as well, with an added component of using an analogy to explain what you think you know.

Chapter 3. Read Faster and Retain More

The previous chapter was about how to cement your understanding of new information. We went through various techniques that are scientifically designed to impart better comprehension and also help you understand what you don't know.

The next step in our learning quest is about reading.

Reading—you've done it since you were a child. What do you have to learn about it? It turns out, you probably have never learned how to read quickly and efficiently. Whatever you've been doing has been adequate to get by, but learning to read better and retain more information is a skill in itself. It's not just the passive absorption of information that you've grown accustomed to.

Chances are, whatever you learn, you will eventually have to read about it. The more you read, the better, which means the faster and more efficiently you read, the faster and more efficient your learning will be. How do we reach that point?

You can often make yourself an expert on an intellectual subject just by reading enough in that area. But despite the incredible importance of reading, most people are wildly inefficient at it. Like a child that never goes beyond a crawl, most people have enough reading skills to move around, but they are far from running.

The average adult reads at a speed of 300 words per minute. You can take various reading and comprehension tests online to test your current abilities if you'd like to discover your word-per-minute rate.

According to a speed-reading test conducted by Staples, here's how many words per minute people read on average:

- Third-grade students:150 wpm
- Eighth-grade students: 250 wpm
- Average adult: 300 wpm
- Average university student: 450 wpm
- Average business executive: 575 wpm
- Average university professor: 675 wpm

Obviously this is not so good for our self-learning quest. Think about the difference if you could add even 100 words more per minute. You would be able to finish a book 25–33% faster. You would be able to spend more time on what matters—analyzing and thinking about the information as opposed to absorbing it. Or you would just finish your reading and spend time on your other pursuits and hobbies.

This chapter will be about teaching you how to read faster, as well as retain more. You will get the best of both worlds. It's important to note that speed-reading as a concept of reading a book in minutes is largely a myth. A few special savants and geniuses in the world may be able to do it, but for the rest of us, our mere mortal brains just can't process things like a computer.

We'll cover four of the top tips in training yourself to read faster while retaining more information at the same time—for mortals. You'll see for yourself (eventually, not immediately!) that speed-reading itself is not a myth, and you can use it in your quest for better learning. What's ahead are the following: how to stop subvocalizing, training your eyes to widen and spread, how to strategically skim for important information, and how to maintain better focus and attention. We'll start with subvocalizations.

Stop Subvocalizations

What are subvocalizations?

When you started to read, you probably read out loud. Your elementary school teacher wanted you to read the book and say the words aloud. After you mastered this skill, you were told to simply say the words inside your head and read quietly.

When it comes to reading, we are often limited by the time that it takes for our subconscious mind to pronounce the words on the page. We don't say them out loud, but our mind speaks them unconsciously: this is known as "subvocalizing." This is where most reading education and skill levels end.

To move to a new level you need to stop sounding the words inside your head. Subvocalizing takes time—more time than is necessary to comprehend the words you are reading. It is almost impossible to go much beyond 400 or 500 words while subvocalizing. And even then, it sounds like you are having a heart attack because you are speaking so fast inside your mind.

When we speak a word out loud, that takes a certain amount of time to pronounce. However, we do not actually need to pronounce words when we read. We can simply absorb them. Instead, you need to train yourself to read without hearing the words in your head.

If someone reads at around a thousand words per minute (entirely possible and trainable), there is no way they could hear the words in their heads while trying to process them. Instead, they simply see the word and their brains extract the meaning of what was written. It's about processing the meaning without speaking the words out loud—this is the essence of stopping subvocalizations and it doesn't sound easy because it's a tough habit to break!

Since most people currently can't separate the subvocalization from comprehension, they are locked in at a rate of about 400–500 words. Moving beyond that rate requires you to embrace that *your mind and eyes read faster than your mouth.*

Start by picking out any word in a paragraph and look at it for a moment in total silence. Look at it, and instead of repeating the word mentally, think about what it represents and means. Think about its meaning. You can even just describe it mentally instead of reading it out loud inside your head. There will still be a slight bit of subvocalization, but by merely observing words without the desire to pronounce them, the new habit will begin to form on its own.

This part might feel obscure or abstract in the beginning, and that's totally normal. It might even feel impossible, and that's natural too because you are fundamentally changing how you take in information. All that you need to be concerned with is looking at words without the desire to hear the way they sound.

Next, pick a sentence somewhere or even write it yourself. Now, instead of subvocalizing when you read it, there are a few things to try to see if they work for you.

First, picture it visually in your mind. Second, hum to yourself as you read it, so you literally can't read it because of the humming. Third, in the same vein, you can practice reading while chewing gum on the same premise that it makes it difficult to subconsciously subvocalize. You are just occupying your inner voice with something else but allowing the processing to occur.

For instance, take a sentence like "The bees are coming." Visualize what that looks like instead of saying the words themselves. That's where you start.

Subvocalizations can be tough to eliminate, but it's pretty clear that you can think faster than you can talk, so you can see how important it is to reading faster.

The next step in reading faster is to train and exercise your eyes—get them into shape for reading faster. Your eyes are muscles too, after all, so you must train them for the bigger workload you are going to give them.

Train Your Eyes

The next major step in learning to read faster and more efficiently is to train your eyes. Your eyes are muscles, so they need to be trained and prepared for reading faster. Obviously it is a bigger workload on your eyes than you are used to. If you read for leisure, your eyes may barely move, but speed-reading is a focus activity that takes time and effort—with big payoffs.

With so-called normal reading, your eyes don't stay fixed in one spot when reading. Eye-tracking studies have shown that your eyes actually quiver and move around considerably. These are called *saccades*. And every movement away from your position in text requires a few milliseconds to readjust and refocus. All of these minuscule readjustments in locating your place in a book add up to be very costly to your reading speed.

So you're not actually training yourself to move your eyes *more*—rather, you are training them to move *less* and in a more controlled way to not waste energy and effort. It's easier than you think, though it might make you feel like you are back in grade school at first.

There are two ways to do this. The first is to use your finger, or any other object, as a pointer. The second is to strengthen your peripheral vision and learn to focus on chunks of words rather than individual words.

Using a finger to guide yourself while reading is often considered to be reserved for children and then forgotten once they have the hang of reading. It's important because it keeps you on track and makes sure you aren't distracted or wasting energy.

This trick comes in handy again while learning to speed-read. Use your index finger to mark where you are on the page at all times. It should follow along with the word you are currently reading, slowly scrolling across each line and then back down one. It may feel awkward at first and it may even temporarily slow your reading rate as you adjust, but using a pointer is critical if you want to improve your reading skill.

By moving your finger faster than you can actually read, your eyes get used to viewing text faster than your brain can process what is written down. This will break your subvocalization attachment and can easily let you increase your reading rate with sufficient practice.

When using a pointer, your primary goal is to move the pointer at a very consistent pace. You should not stop your finger or slow it down. It should simply slide from one side of the text to the other at a very uniform speed.

Go ahead and try it right now with any writing that is in front of you. You can even pause this lesson for a minute to try it. You might feel silly, but you'll find that using a finger will focus your eye movements and even push you to a faster speed.

One of the biggest and easiest epiphanies in your journey to becoming a speed-reader will be in recognizing how much your eyes move while you read. For the average person, their eyes cannot keep moving in a single, fluid line without needing to backtrack. If you begin to pay attention to your eyes, I can guarantee that you will start to notice just how often you move back, then forward, then back again. In the long run, this adds entire hours to your reading experience, and it might even prevent you from finishing in the first place.

The second part of exercising your eyes, besides using a pointer and calming your excess eye movements, is to deal with *eye fixation*. An eye fixation is a location on the page where your eye comes to a stop. Readers who make fewer eye fixations read faster because they take in more words with each fixation.

The wider your vision span, the more words you can process in an eye fixation and the faster you can read—and, of course, the fewer eye fixations you make on any given page. So to deal with eye fixation, we must widen how much we can see at one time, basically. Acquiring the ability to see many words at a time is essential for speed-reading. The goal is to stop looking at a single word at a time and instead start learning how to look at chunks of words.

You are trying to strengthen your peripheral vision. *Macular vision* is your primary focus. When you look directly at something, you see with your macular vision. *Peripheral vision* is what you see less distinctly in the area outside your macular vision. Because receptor cells on the retina of your eye are concentrated at the center and are less concentrated toward the edges, colors and shapes are harder to distinguish in peripheral vision (although you can quickly pick up on motion).

But you can see to the left, to the right, above, and below the area bordered by your macular vision. The point is, your peripheral vision needs to improve to read faster and reduce eye fixations, so exercise your eyes to do this.

There are six muscles attached to each of your eyes. These muscles control all of the movements your eyes make, including the movements that make your eyes look up, down, and all around. Eye muscles also help your eyes focus on near objects and objects far away. Just like any other muscle in your body, exercise helps your eye muscles gain strength and flexibility. And just like other muscles, there are specially designed exercises that help build eye muscle strength and flexibility.

Here is a simple eye exercise designed to help build eye muscle flexibility and enhance your reading speed.

To start, sit or stand and focus your vision straight ahead. Next stretch each hand out to the side like you used to do when pretending you were an airplane. Stick each thumb up toward the sky and hold that pose.

Now, keeping your head straight, move your eyes to the right until you can see your thumb. If you can't quite see it, just stretch your eyes as far to the right side as you can. Then glance to the left while making sure you keep your head still and facing straight ahead. This is one repetition. Try not to move your head, only your eyes, so you are stretching your eyes to each side and working the muscles involved.

Continue glancing right to left and left to right nine more times. That is one set of 10 repetitions. Repeat the sequence of 10 glances to each side for a total of three sets. Your eyes should feel pretty tired at the end of it; it will be a weird and unfamiliar feeling.

It doesn't seem like it, but this act of stretching and working your eye muscles will widen your sphere of vision. Where you previously could only focus on one word, you now have the ability to visually focus on two or three. As your peripheral eye muscles get stronger, you might even evolve to seeing an entire line of text in one glance. The point is, if you only double yourself by seeing two words at a time, you have effectively doubled your reading speed just by training your eyes. This technique, along with using a pointer finger or object, will hugely aid you in better reading.

The next step in reading better is about strategically skimming information and how to draw out the important parts by knowing what to look for and what you can skip.

Strategically Skim

The next step in reading faster is to understand how to strategically skim your material—after stopping subvocalizations and training your eyes. For most of us, skimming has a negative connotation. It's when we are rushed for time and can only look at the first sentence of each paragraph—or whatever method you decide makes sense. This is not the same type of skimming.

Frankly, not all information is created equally, and this can be true even within sentences and paragraphs. There are some things that are destined to waste our time in reading, so we should learn exactly what is okay to skip, what to focus on, and how to manage all of that. Skimming information in our context is about saving time and being able to see through what's in front of you.

Here, we are skimming in a way that lets you retain just as much, just by cutting the fat. Traditional skimming would be skipping about 75% of the content—here, we are only skipping 25% of the content.

How are we doing that? There are three interrelated methods.

First, start and stop reading three words from the margin of the pages.

By default, we always start reading the first word on the left of the page and go all the way to the last word on the right. We've been taught to be thorough and leave no stone unturned. But here's the trick: you can start on the third word from the left and stop three words from the end, and your peripheral vision just might pick up the first two and last two words automatically.

In a line of 10 words, this allows you to "read" only six words and save 40% of the effort and time. This obviously adds up quite quickly. As with all these techniques, stop the course and try it for a second. Does it feel odd? Does it feel like you are skipping important information? Just try it out and you'll find that you aren't missing anything for comprehension—your brain will fill it in, and you'll be able to figure it out through the context of the sentence.

Second, skip *meaningless* words.

To be clear, skipping small words isn't quite the same thing as skimming what you're reading. When you skim, you're not retaining the words or ideas that you're consuming. You may have a general sense of the work, but the fine details will likely be lost.

Learning how to read faster is all about eliminating the small, unnecessary words that fill up a page. Not every word is created equal. There are plenty of small, obscure little words that don't help you, and trying to force yourself to read them can only hurt. These words certainly have their place, of course, and we need them to construct sentences and ideas! But when we're trying to read quickly, we can often skip these words with no ill-effects: "if," "is," "to," "the," "and," "was."

The best part of skipping the small words is that they do not contribute anything useful, so skipping them effectively means that you are getting more out of your reading experience in less time. If you are reading a fiction or poetry book and you want to appreciate the prose and sentence structure, this tip may not work for you. But then again, you wouldn't be trying to read those books quickly anyway!

Let's look at an example sentence that uses some of those useless words. "**The** dog went inside **the** house, **and** ate his dinner, which **was** leftover spaghetti." How many words can you eliminate from that sentence? At least four or five. The sentence is 14 words. That's one-third of the sentence!

Third, scan for *important* words. This is related to the previous point of ignoring useless words. When you can identify what matters in a sentence, that understanding is all that is needed. As you read any given sentence, you will probably get 90% of the meaning from 50% of the words, and for the purposes of learning at a quick pace, the rest of the words are unnecessary filler.

For example, "I went to the vet yesterday because my cat was sick." That is an 11-word sentence.

What are the important words in that sentence? "Vet," "yesterday," "cat," and "sick." There are only four words in the sentence, and everything else isn't necessary to get the meaning. You can absolutely get the meaning of the sentence just from those words. This is easier to do than the previous step and also allows you to save more time from the so-called meaningless and useless words.

Let's have another easy example. "I want to go to China because I hear the food is very tasty and the people are nice."

How many words do you really need to get the meaning in that sentence? "Want," "go," "China," "food," "tasty," "people," and "nice." That's seven words out of 19 words for the sentence. You can see how valuable this method can be.

Scanning paragraphs like this takes practice, but it can greatly increase your reading speed. And the beauty is that if you scan through a paragraph and don't completely grasp the meaning, you just go back, slow down, and add the words back in until it makes sense. Then take off again.

Strategically skimming information is probably not what you initially thought it was. Most people think of skimming as quickly going through information and missing all the vital parts. But here, skimming is learning how to parse information and only read what is needed to get the meaning and understanding. It's tougher but very rewarding in your path to learning better and reading faster.

The final part of reading faster is how to gain focus and attention and ignore distractions.

Focus and Attention

It should go without saying that reading is not something you can multitask. It requires all of your attention and focus. Sadly, most of us don't treat reading with the respect it deserves, and that is why we often find ourselves reading through the same paragraph over and over again. How can we improve our focus when it comes to reading in particular?

This final section is about maintaining your focus and not letting these other techniques be wasted if you simply can't pay attention to your materials!

First, eliminate distractions. There will always be distractions out of your control, but we're more concerned with distractions that are *in* your control. Avoid unplanned and unwelcome distractions.

For example, if your phone starts ringing while you're reading, this is a distraction that is in your control and you can eliminate it. Just turn your phone off for the time that you'll be reading. If you have the constant urge to check your email or Facebook while you read, then try turning your computer off while you read. If other people constantly interrupt you, then you may want to try reading in a different location. These are all distractions that can be controlled. And if they can be controlled, we should eliminate them to achieve a higher level of focus while reading.

What other distractions are within your control? Well, almost everything you surround yourself with in your physical environment. That's a start. Next, you can proactively tell people not to distract you during a time period—they may not know that you are trying to focus, so you can prevent their unplanned distracting presence.

Second, create a game. How fast can you read a page of text while still maintaining a high level of comprehension? Why not time yourself and try to beat your record one page at a time?

Remember what it was like to be a kid? Everything was a game! Remember how long you used to stay focused on playing with a toy or a game that you found interesting? When we grew up, we forgot that we could turn anything into a game.

Games motivate us and engage parts of the brain tied to our need for entertainment and challenge. By creating little games with our reading material, we can trick our brains into thinking we are playing a game instead of engaging in the laborious task of reading. Oftentimes we read through boring material with diligence because it can mean the difference between a passing and failing grade in school or not getting our job done at work. All this does is burn us out. At one point in my life, it made me hate reading in general.

All we have to do is change our perspective on the material and mimic the joy of reading something we are actually interested in. This will make reading a lot more fluid and effortless, and you could create your own reading utopia where even the most boring material is still fun to read. All you need to do is have a stopwatch or watch, and you can attempt to see how much you can write, absorb, or read every five or 10 minutes. Rinse and repeat, and make it a game to compete with yourself. You may find that the game is motivating you to focus your attention better.

Third, make sure you take breaks. Peter Drucker, the father of business management, talks in his book *The Effective Executive* about how 50-minute chunks of time are ideal for focusing on a single task. This is because 50 minutes is the ideal amount of time to focus on one item before we start to require a break. Something happens after we go beyond the 50-minute mark. Our brain starts to become more inefficient. It's then time for a 10-minute break. After the break, you can focus on reading for another 50 minutes. By using this cycle, not only will you get the most out of reading, but you will also be able to train your focus and develop the habit of working at a specific pace.

Make sure to take breaks after at most every 50 minutes, otherwise your brain will start losing focus and you will slowly start to reread each sentence or paragraph a few times before absorbing it. The point is that you need a break, whether you read for only 25 minutes or up to 50 minutes. Think of the brain as a muscle—an athlete needs to rest his muscles while training, and so do you.

Learning to read isn't difficult—we've all done it. But learning to read with a purpose, and how to do it optimally, might be completely new to you. Treat it with the attention it deserves and it will greatly help your learning in general.

Reading faster is a huge component of learning better. If most of how you learn is through the written word, it's clear that you should learn to deal with it faster and more efficiently.

"How to Read a Book"

Did you know that there are four levels of reading?

The four levels of reading were developed by philosopher Mortimer Adler in his suitably titled publication *How to Read a Book*. Adler explains that reading is not a single, universally consistent act. He breaks up the act of reading into four individual levels that differ in purpose, effort, and the amount of time it takes. Furthermore, different tiers apply to different kinds of reading—some books can be appropriate for all levels, while others just support one or two. Especially in the higher two levels, faithfully following these tiers of reading will greatly advance your expertise on the subject. When you pair this kind of comprehension with speed-reading, you can become a learning machine.

These are Adler's four levels of reading, from simplest to most complex:

- elementary

- inspectional

- analytical

- syntopical

Elementary. You're already past this level— this is, essentially, learning to read. It's the kind of reading that's taught in elementary school. You're learning what the letters are, how words are pronounced, and what they objectively mean. It's knowing that the sentence "The cat is on the bed" means there's a cat on the bed and that it *doesn't* say there's a dog on the couch. Blows the mind, right?

The elementary stage also applies to an adult who's learning a new language and has to be trained to understand new alphabets, vocabulary, and pronunciation. It also applies to a student reading a technical textbook for the first time and has to learn new syntax or specific jargon. Anytime you come upon a new language, dialect, or lexicon, you're doing elementary reading.

Inspectional. The next level up for readers is understanding the essence of a certain book—but not digesting the whole of it. It's called the inspectional stage, and it's sometimes disparaged or discounted by avid readers. But in developing expertise, it's a very valuable process.

Inspectional reading actually has two mini-stages of its own:

- *Systematic skimming.* This is casually examining certain elements of a book apart from the body of the text: skimming the table of contents and the index or reading the preface or the blurb on the inside jacket. If you're assessing an e-book, it could mean reading the online description and customer reviews as well. Systematic skimming gives you enough information to know what the book is and how you would classify it: "it's a novel about World War II" or "it's a book that explains how to cook French cuisine." That's it.

- *Superficial reading.* This stage is actually reading the book but in a very casual way. You start at the beginning and take in the material without consuming it or thinking too much about it. You don't make notes in the margins. You don't look up unfamiliar phrases or concepts—if there's a passage you don't understand, you just proceed to the next part. In superficial reading, you're getting a sense of the tone, rhythm, and general direction of the book rather than absorbing every single element of the narrative.

Inspectional reading is something like a recon mission or a survey. You're just getting a sense of what the book is about and the reading experience. You might pick up on a couple of very broad, general ideas in the book, but you won't go very deeply into them. You'll just find out what you might be in for, and then you'll decide whether you're interested enough to go more in-depth.

For example, let's say you're looking at a book on classical music. In your systematic skimming, you'd see the title and subtitle. You'd read the back flap, which says it's "an in-depth but gently irreverent study of classical composers." You'd read the table of contents—there are chapters entitled "Wagner in Drag," "Mozart's Cat Imitations," and "Beethoven's Love of Rats." At this point, you've probably ascertained that this is *not* a terribly serious work and not one that's likely to add to your expertise, although it may be entertaining.

Why should a budding expert go through this stage and not just skip to the next level? Even though it's not a deep dive, it gives you a lot of answers. You'll get a sense of the writer's approach: is it serious, comical, or satirical? Does it rely on real-life accounts or imaginary situations? Is it heavy on statistics? Does it quote a lot of outside sources? Are there pictures?

Having a good sense of the answers to those questions will help you frame the content and define your expectations, which—if you've decided to proceed with the book—will make the next level of reading more productive.

Analytical. The third level of reading is the deepest level for consuming a single book or volume of work—it's full digestion of *and interaction with* the material at hand. The challenge of analytical reading is simply this: "If time's not an object, how thoroughly would you read this book?"

Analytical reading can be described as taking the book out of the author's hands and making it your own. You don't just read the text; you highlight or underline key points and you make commentary or ask questions. In a way, you can use the marginalia to simulate an ongoing conversation with the writer.

The goal of analytical reading is to understand the material well enough so you can explain it to someone else without a lot of effort. You're able to describe the subject very concisely. You're able to list its parts in order and say how they connect with each other. You're able to understand and specify the issues the writer's concerned with and what problems they're trying to resolve.

For example, if you're reading Stephen Hawking's *A Brief History of Time*, you'd highlight key phrases in the first part about the history of physics: the Big Bang theory, black holes, and time travel, for example. You might asterisk the names of Copernicus and Galileo with a note to research them more fully. You might question Hawking's explanation of the expanding universe with writing in the margins.

Analytical reading is hard work. But it's the level at which the thrill of gaining new understanding is most profound and rewarding. This kind of interaction with reading makes learning proactive—instead of just listening to what some person's telling you, it's more like you're extracting the information yourself. When you're doing that, you're engaging more of your mind, and that means it's far more likely you're going to *remember* what you've learned. That's a much easier path toward expertise.

Syntopical. In the final level of reading, you work with multiple books or pieces of material covering the same subject. One could describe syntopical reading as "compare/contrast," but it's actually a lot deeper than that. (And syntopical reading is not to be confused with the similarly spelled *synoptical* reading, which is pretty much its exact opposite.)

At this stage, you're trying to understand the entire breadth of the subject you're studying, not just a single volume about it. Sound familiar? You analyze the differences in the ideas, syntax, and arguments presented in the books and compare them. You're able to identify and fill any gaps in knowledge you might have. You're conversing with multiple partners and forming and arranging the most pressing questions you need to answer. You're identifying all the issues and aspects of the subjects that the books cover and looking up phraseology and vocabulary that you don't understand.

Syntopical reading is a relatively major commitment, almost like a semester-long college course you're teaching yourself. Think of it as an active effort, something one doesn't normally associate with the relaxing act of reading a novel.

It's like a TV show or movie in which someone's trying to unravel a multilayered criminal enterprise. Somewhere in the movie, they show a giant bulletin board in the station with drawings, Post-its, and pictures of people, with pieces of yarn showing how they're all interconnected. When new information is discovered from different sources, it all gets added to that board. That's what syntopical reading is like: it's a concerted effort to find the answers and increase your expertise, and you don't even have to deal with the mob. You can concentrate on more lawful subjects like Occam's Razor, absurdist theatre, or the stock market.

These four levels serve as connected steps that gradually make a subject approachable, more relevant, and, finally, fully familiar to you.

In the elementary stage, well, you're learning to read. You kind of need that for everything.

In the inspectional phase, you're getting an overview of the framework and structure and gauging your interest. You're priming yourself in case you decide to commit to the analytical phase by estimating what's in store for you at a deeper level.

In the analytical phase, you're committing to an extensive effort to understand as much of the subject as you can from as many viewpoints as possible. You're absorbing and questioning the book and creating further curiosity about the topic it addresses, driving yourself to learn more.

In the syntopical phase, you've "graduated," in a sense, from a single or limited perspective of the subject to a holistic study of all its elements. This point is where you're layering the levels of your expertise at multiple points—something you can't even comprehend in typically casual or recreational reading.

Some of the processes in this chapter might seem daunting or impossible at first glance. But remember this: at some point in every expert's life, they knew *nothing* about what they've become experts about. Whether they learned in educational institutions or on their own, they went through a period when they had to gather information in a vacuum and take a deep dive into unfamiliar waters. You are absolutely capable of doing exactly what these experts had to do. In fact, you may have it a little easier than they did and can find your path to expertise simpler to follow than you thought.

Takeaways:

- This chapter is geared toward imparting how to read faster and also retain more information at the same time. It sounds like a tall task, but it's unlikely you've learned much about reading since when you were learning the alphabet—that is to say, not much. There are a few important aspects to reading faster.

- You must stop subvocalizations. This is when you mentally read words out loud. You can think and process faster than you can read out loud. This means instead of sounding out and pronouncing words, you must imagine their meaning in their place. It's a tough habit to break.

- Second, you must train your eyes. After all, each eye has six muscles that control its movements. You must train your eyes in two ways: to move less and to look wider with peripheral vision.

- Third, you must learn how to strategically skim by avoiding useless words, focusing on important words, and ignoring words at the edge of the pages.

- Finally, you must learn how your focus and attention works in regard to reading. Give it the respect it deserves and take scheduled breaks, make games to read faster, and eliminate distractions.

- How do you read a book? A final section details the four levels of reading as articulated by author Mortimer Adler. The levels are elementary, inspectional, analytical, and syntopical. Most of us only get through the first two levels and don't engage with the material and have a conversation with it. That's where deep, true comprehension comes from.

Chapter 4. Skills and Habits to Teach Yourself Anything

Sometimes you know that there's a gap in your knowledge and that there's a question you have to ask that will clarify the information for you, but for whatever reason, you don't ask the question. Of course, that's in best-case scenarios when you even realize that something is askew.

For me, this usually happened in math classes in elementary school. Back in first grade—or so I was told—I made a fairly common mistake when it came to using rulers. The teacher asked us to use our rulers to draw lines of two, four, and six inches long. So I took out my ruler, put the pencil on the "1" spot, and drew a line to the numbers "2," "4," and "6." When I saw what I'd drawn, something seemed off compared to what my classmates had drawn. But I figured I'd done what I was asked and turned the paper in without asking the teacher about it. The truth was, I was in a rush to get out to recess and make sure my spot in the handball line was secured.

But as an adult, you probably spotted my error. I started at "1," because that was the number I always started counting at. But I should have started at "0." I *knew* something was off but didn't seek to clarify the instructions. I got all three answers wrong. After I returned from recess, my day was ruined, other children laughed at me, and I ate lunch grumpily and in silence.

Of course, there's a difference between a first grader who's still learning *how* to learn and an adult who's had plenty of experience in learning. But this shameful example from my past demonstrates one of the many habits and skills associated with self-learning: asking questions. It's not as simple as asking for facts, and it is indeed something that must be cultivated like any other skill.

But when we take on the task of self-education, it's almost like having to adjust to a new way of learning. We have to tinker with our learning strategy as we shift from someone else teaching us to driving the teaching ourselves. This chapter covers some of the adjustments an aspiring self-learner can make to ensure they get the most out of their studies. First up, we'll talk about how to create plans for learning.

Plans, Schedules, and Goals

One historical figure who provides a fantastic example of how to create goals and plan yourself to success is none other than Benjamin Franklin. He's still the supreme example of an autodidact: a statesman, inventor, philosopher, writer, and polymath whose curiosity knew no limits.

Franklin was fastidious about keeping track of his goals, activities, and schedules, and he used them to navigate his personal and professional life. Two of his daily techniques for arranging his life are perfect for those looking to improve their organizational skills for better learning. Both were laid out in detail in Franklin's autobiography, perhaps with the hope of inspiring future generations to similar levels of achievement and productivity.

The first and probably more famous of Franklin's forms is his "13 virtues" checklist, which he used to chart his efforts in bettering himself as a human being. Although he used the 13 virtues for self-improvement—or, as Franklin put it, "attaining moral perfection"—they serve as a strong example of how to mindfully track progress and keep records of anything you want to develop, including self-learning.

First, Franklin devised a list of 13 qualities he felt he needed to develop in order to live a healthy and conscientious life when he was 20 years old (a freakishly young age to display such maturity, if you ask me). They included merits (not relevant to this chapter's discussion but helpful for illustration):

1. **Temperance**. Eat not to dullness; drink not to elevation.
2. **Silence**. Speak not but what may benefit others or yourself; avoid trifling conversation.
3. **Order**. Let all your things have their places; let each part of your business have its time.
4. **Resolution**. Resolve to perform what you ought; perform without fail what you resolve.
5. **Frugality**. Make no expense but to do good to others or yourself; i.e., waste nothing.
6. **Industry**. Lose no time; be always employ'd in something useful; cut off all unnecessary actions.
7. **Sincerity**. Use no hurtful deceit; think innocently and justly, and, if you speak, speak accordingly.
8. **Justice**. Wrong none by doing injuries, or omitting the benefits that are your duty.

9. **Moderation**. Avoid extremes; forbear resenting injuries so much as you think they deserve.
10. **Cleanliness**. Tolerate no uncleanliness in body, clothes, or habitation.
11. **Tranquillity**. Be not disturbed at trifles, or at accidents common or unavoidable.
12. **Chastity**. Rarely use venery but for health or offspring, never to dullness, weakness, or the injury of your own or another's peace or reputation.
13. **Humility**. Imitate Jesus and Socrates.

He then devised a system by which he strove to improve in each area in a very deliberate, methodical way. Coming up with the idea for the list itself is revolutionary in a way, since it focused his attention on what he was trying to accomplish. It was also a tall task—how many goals are you currently working on right now? Is it anywhere close to 13? It's time to rethink what is possible.

Franklin drew up a series of cards, each of which contained a very simple table with seven columns and 13 rows. Heading each column were the seven days of the week:

Sunday through Saturday. At the head of each row were symbols for each of his 13 virtues. At the top of the entire page, Franklin wrote down the virtue that he chose to pay particular attention to for the duration of the week. The first week, he chose to focus primarily on temperance.

At the end of each day of the week, Franklin took out this card, reviewed the matrix, and put a black dot in each square for every instance during the day that he felt he "fell short" of maintaining that virtue. For example, if he felt he'd had a few too many glasses of wine at a Thursday dinner, he'd put a black dot in the "temperance" box for Thursday. If he decided he'd gotten a little too ticked off at George Washington at a Saturday meeting, he might put a black dot in the Saturday "tranquility" box.

In any given week, Franklin primarily focused on the virtue he entered at the top of each card. His reasoning was that cultivating one virtue at a time would make next week's virtue a little easier to handle and that each virtue would become a habit in time. Each virtue was carefully scheduled

129

so that one week's virtue would help inform the next week's—for example, he put "frugality" the week before "industry" because he thought the habit of saving money would inform his habit of working harder to obtain money. One at a time ensured that he wouldn't be overwhelmed and could discover what it took him to change a singular aspect of his life.

After Franklin had worked his way through 13 weeks of checklists, he'd start over and begin a new series with his top virtue. He repeated all of his virtue exercises as he needed. If he faithfully did it every week, that meant he'd perform the task four times a year (13 weeks × 4 = 52 weeks = 1 year). Really, you just have to stand back and admire how neatly Franklin worked a calendar.

The genius of Franklin's checklist is that this approach works for other things besides becoming a better human being (though that's certainly a fine pursuit to try). Intentional planning, honest self-monitoring, and devotion of time without distraction is the name of the game.

For many of us still, this is a level of attention and self-awareness that is unheard of. We tend to think of our behavior as inborn and relatively unchangeable—but that's not the case if you don't want it to be the case, like Franklin. This type of intentional development and improvement underlay his success and accomplishments. You can also use it to track progress and chart your tasks in anything, including individual subjects of self-learning.

For example, if you're teaching yourself about the Spanish language and culture, you might come up with a few "planks" of your studies that you want to make sure you cover as much as possible: "reading," "writing," "audio practice," "social studies," "music/art," and so on. It might not make sense to cover each of these areas every single day (or maybe it would), but at least a certain number of times each week would be helpful. Instead of focusing on a "Virtue of the Week" as Franklin did, maybe you'd pick a certain aspect of Spanish studies to focus on—"food," "history," "politics," "sport," "art," "manners"—whatever you know you'll be covering and could organize in a weekly cadence.

The key to this system's success is knowing what aspects of your studies are the most important to maintain—the same way Franklin decided what virtues were most essential for him to build on. Each subject will have different areas of importance. Separate them out and organize a plan of attack toward them that ensures that all your bases are covered. Your brain can only handle so many things at once, so plan yourself out of overwhelm and multitasking. Progress and learning in any regard require a steady march, even one that is tracked by weeks and years as Franklin's 13 virtues were.

Don't just do what you *feel* like or whatever pops into your mind—be methodical and make sure nothing slips through the cracks. This is the purpose of the syllabus and schedule for a class in traditional education—be sure to create your own to keep yourself on track and be an effective self-learner.

As Franklin himself noted, the real value of this system is to instill better habits on a rolling, gradual basis. Any kind of study system is extremely dependent on how well you nurture positive habits, and this is exceptionally true with self-learning since you're in charge of monitoring *everything*.

But we're not done with Benjamin Franklin yet, the famed proponent of the turkey as the national bird of the United States. How did he manage to accomplish so many great things in an almost countless number of areas?

The second part of his planning genius stems from the daily schedule he kept for himself. In his biography, Franklin also took the time to map out his schedule for each day, from waking up to bedtime. For example, one of his typical schedules (partially paraphrased) looked like this:

- *5:00 a.m. to 8:00 a.m.*: Rise, wash, "address powerful goodness" (pray or meditate), schedule the day, "prosecute the present study" (study and research whatever projects he was pursuing besides work), eat breakfast.

- *8:00 a.m. to 12:00 p.m.*: Work.

- *12:00 p.m. to 2:00 p.m.*: Read, "overlook my accounts" (attend to his personal or financial business), eat lunch.

- *2:00 p.m. to 5:00 p.m.*: Work.

- *5:00 p.m. to 10:00 p.m.*: Reflect, eat supper, consider "what good" he'd done during the day, enjoy "diversion" like hobbies, music, or conversation.

- *10:00 p.m. to 5:00 a.m.*: Sleep.

This may not look like an especially precise schedule in comparison to the schedules we may keep today, considering the infinite numbers of appointments and meetings we tend to fill our calendars with. But it's a great example to follow because it allows room for everything necessary to one's mental well-being: it treats personal and recreational activities with the exact same importance as business and work. Everything he did was directed: it had its proper time and context, and all his activities were vital to his development the same way his virtues were. In an ideal world, a schedule focused on self-learning wouldn't look too different.

Franklin also differentiated between work he had to focus on exclusively (in those bigger morning and afternoon chunks) and work he could do while he was doing something else, like overlooking his accounts and conducting his personal studies. That undoubtedly gave him some flexibility and ease when he could take care of affairs that were important but could be done at a less active pace among the other relaxing things he did, like lunching. Actually scheduling time for personal reflection—something most of us probably don't think to do—shows that he realized it was both a vital activity to pursue *and* that it had its place during the day, no more or less important than anything else on his docket.

Even with his somewhat slower pace of life (compared to our own, that is), Franklin didn't always strictly keep to his schedule.

That's fine. I'm sure in his day, like our own, things just *came up*. The benefit of having that daily plan was that it made him happier to at least *try* to live according to a schedule. If he didn't have even an *idea* of what he wanted to accomplish on a certain day, he'd be lost.

Having a schedule helped him feel more organized and productive, even if he didn't follow it 100% every single day. Simply having something to refer to with premade decisions can lend guidance and structure to a day that wouldn't exist otherwise. You see, it's when we are faced with decisions that we run into problems. Once you remove the presence of decisions with a detailed schedule, you are far more likely to go along with what needs to happen.

So using Franklin's overall concept for your own schedule, here are some guidelines you should follow:

- Give yourself a couple of daily blocks to focus on your primary work. But give yourself as much flexibility within those blocks to mentally wander. Large blocks of time are more forgiving and allow you the space to go where the wind takes you.

- Schedule some time for recreation, leisure, personal reflection, or socializing with family and friends. Franklin knew these aspects were crucial enough to make room for them, especially personal reflection and understanding what went well and what needed to change during the day. The brain can't run on full speed all the time.

- Treat your personal goals with the same respect as your professional goals—in other words, schedule your self-learning with the same priority as your other responsibilities.

- Spend a relatively equal amount of time planning, ruminating, analyzing, and preparing as you do actually taking action. What went well and what didn't? Make sure you're doing the *right* thing instead of the *easy* thing and that you learn from your mistakes and inefficiencies.

- Wash. Definitely find time to wash.

These two habits of Benjamin Franklin—creating overarching goals and plans and adhering to a daily schedule—are habits we can emulate. Self-learning isn't something you can wing; planning is paramount to self-learning because it is inherently tedious and boring and sometimes you just can't give yourself the choice to not. Take a cue from this famous founding father and protect yourself from your worst impulses.

The structures of long-range planning and schedules make it easier for us to achieve our goals. This brings us to the next question—what were those goals again? Attempting to set goals like Benjamin Franklin's 13 virtues probably won't work for us, for numerous and varied reasons. So how can we use goals to plan ourselves into better self-learning?

The first guideline is to accept that *you don't really know what you don't know yet, and you're not going to find out until you finally know it*. In self-learning—frankly, in any ambitious goal—you'll often be coming face to face with the unknown. It's uncomfortable at best. You need to understand that and not let it scare you off from making the goal, because that's exactly what it does to a lot of us. Your goal is to learn things you don't know, anyway. It will inevitably feel like a challenge.

But you should make sure it is just the right amount of challenge for the right moment. You should try to establish goals that are realistically achievable and not so easy that achieving them won't make you feel a sense of accomplishment. They shouldn't be outrageously pie-in-the-sky goals that would be impossible in the short term, but they should be something you haven't done before. Maybe just a *tiny* bit higher than you think you can do, but not too high as to discourage you. There's a sweet spot as to how the goals you set can keep you motivated.

For instance, if we apply this to Benjamin Franklin, we can say that he probably felt that attempting to master 20 virtues at once was too difficult and decided an attainable challenge would *be* 13 virtues—yet he felt that attempting to master nine virtues would be *settling*. Everyone has different levels of what challenges them, and it's up to us to set goals that keep us moving toward them.

Of course, for our purposes, these goals should be related to self-learning. If you want to learn French, utilize a goal that will enforce self-learning, such as having a casual conversation at a café. Learn 120 words if you imagine you can only learn 100—when in reality you are undervaluing your own skills. If you want to learn the violin, set a goal in learning a piece by your favorite composer, even if it is above your skill level. Learn the piece in two weeks and create a self-fulfilling prophecy by way of the goal you set.

One handy mnemonic device that can help guide your goal-setting is the SMART acronym. When you've come up with a goal for learning, evaluate it to ensure how it meets five standards—that your goal is the following:

- **S**pecific: clear and definitive

- **M**easurable: easy for you to track progress

- **A**chievable: within your reach but not too simple

- **R**elevant: personally significant to you and your life

- **T**ime-based: organized to some kind of schedule

For example, let's say you're planning on teaching yourself piano. If somebody asks you about it, you could say something like, "I'm going to teach myself everything about piano. By the end of this year I'm going to be a virtuoso with amazing piano skills who can play anything and everything by ear."

That would be a tad on the unrealistic side. Instead, use the SMART filters. Make your goal clearer and attainable:

Specific: "I'm going to learn music theory for piano and get to the point where I can understand and play basic sheet music."

Measurable: "I'm going to learn how to play 10 pieces on piano."

Achievable: "They're going to be somewhat uncomplicated pieces, not overly complex classical pieces, but something I think I can manage before I decide to take the next step."

Relevant: "I'm doing this because I'm a fan of music and I really want to transfer my passion into making art."

Time-based: "I'm giving myself a year from now, practicing and learning at least 10 hours a week."

Using the SMART guidelines to craft your goals will help you think about them more sensibly and practically. If you can center your planning on self-education goals that you can obtain with the resources you currently have, it will give you a better point of view and structure for the course you're learning—and the courses you'll take in the future.

Asking Questions and Pulling Information

With your scheduling, planning, and goal-setting methods in place, you're ready to build the framework of what you're going to learn. The rubber is about ready to hit the road as you start cataloging your resources for your selected subject. And this is exactly the point where you can start getting overwhelmed in your self-learning strategy.

These days, information is extremely easy to find and accumulate. Every subject under the sun is well-represented by online resources and public libraries, and information is going to come to you both through your self-guided efforts and from out of the blue.

But all this information isn't going to *teach* you by itself. All it will do is *present* itself. The data you get doesn't necessarily explain its significance, its context, or meaning. When you're teaching yourself, you won't have a mentor always in place to explain the implications or value or what you're learning, because the structure is all up to you.

So you'll have to be proactive about figuring out what all this new data means to your course of study. You'll have to do the investigative work to understand the framework and substance of all these bits of knowledge. We call this *pulling* information, because it means dragging what's important and creating significance out of the huge mass of info that's just been plopped down in front on you.

Questions are the tools that you'll use to decipher and analyze all this information. But not all questions are created equal. You need questions to develop open avenues of perception and full comprehension of your subject—not just the surface details or dry facts. The questions you'll ask will penetrate far beyond simple common knowledge and will fill in the complete picture of what you're studying.

This is commonly known as critical thinking, and it's the act of delaying gratification in lieu of accuracy and a three-dimensional understanding of the nuances presented to you. It's not terribly popular as a way of navigating life, but it's how you are going to learn to pull information out of your sources.

The goal of critical thinking isn't to produce a quick, easily digestible answer. In fact, it's not even to provide any certifiable conclusion whatsoever. Instead, the point of critical thinking is to increase your mental engagement with a certain topic. Rather than provide a rock-solid, inarguable conviction, critical thinking merely expands your viewpoint and gives you several ways to look at a situation or problem. It gets you past the external noise and easy answers to show you the whole scope of a circumstance or issue. No course of self-learning can succeed without critical thinking.

The questions you use in critical thinking go beyond standard "just the facts, ma'am" inquiries. Instead they challenge the answerer to probe the reasons for a subject's importance, its origins, relevance, and countering or alternative beliefs. They can be applied to any subject—even, with some adaptation, scientific or mathematical principles. The goal isn't to get you to agree or disagree with a given doctrine, but just to understand the totality of its meaning.

Let's try an example: *Keynesian economics.* All that you need to know about it is that it endorses the theory that increased government spending and decreased taxes are how economies can rally themselves out of depression and stimulate growth. It's tricky to discuss it without ruffling some political feathers, but that's a good reason to use it as an example of how to objectively question a topic.

Here are some questions you could use to critically evaluate the topic. I'm not going to attempt to answer them, because last time I checked, I wasn't an economist. But I did look up enough to form some decent questions, and the main point of this exercise is to show they can be phrased:

What makes Keynesian economics important? This question, obviously, seeks out why Keynesian economics are a "thing" and deserve to be talked about.

Which details of Keynesian economics are important and why? This question gets down into the specific elements of

Keynesian theory and how they affect certain specific factors of an economy.

What are the differences between Keynesian economics and classical economics? This sets up a comparison of two different models or problem-solving methods and allows you to understand what sets one model apart from the other.

How is Keynesian economics related to fiscal government policy? This question sets up a description of how the subject relates to other forces.

What evidence can you provide for or against Keynesian economics? This question forces both positive and negative aspects of the subject. Each subject or topic has weaknesses and strengths regarding its applicability and universality.

What patterns do you notice in Keynesian economics? This helps you seek repetitive elements and cause-and-effect relationships, which almost always indicate importance.

What are the advantages and disadvantages of Keynesian economics? This question sets up another comparison between the possible effects of Keynesian economics.

When might Keynesian economics be most useful and why? This question seeks an example of how the concept is used in the real world and can affect your life.

What criteria would you use to assess whether Keynesian economics are successful? This question seeks how to establish hard proof that a concept is working or not and introduces the concept of specific metrics.

What information would you need to make a decision about Keynesian economics? This question addresses the conditions in which Keynesian models can thrive and generally what contextual information is important.

What might happen if you combined Keynesian economics and supply-side economics? This question poses how the concept would flourish or fail when combined with aspects of an alternative model.

What ideas could you add to Keynesian economics and how would these ideas change it? This question challenges you to come up with your own educated ideas and project how they would change the concept.

Do you agree that Keynesian economics work? Why or why not? This question encourages you to use your own reasoning to judge the merit of a certain concept.

What solutions could you suggest to the problem of Keynesian economics? Which might be most effective and why? Similarly, this question calls upon you to reason what could potentially improve the theory.

How could you create or design a new model of Keynesian economics? Explain your thinking. This question encourages you to reimagine the concept in accordance with your own ideas and project how they could work in the future.

Whew. That's a lot of questions. It's only a fraction of the many sides and angles from which you can examine any given issue. None of them are answered in definitive terms, nor can they be. But their open-ended nature encourages you to pursue the facts from an objective standpoint. Is this beginning to sound circular and repetitive? It can indeed be a never-ending and tedious exercise, but if you keep the purpose of discovery and perspective at the forefront, it seems more meaningful.

At this point you may have used all your answers to formulate a theory or conclusion—or you've come across conclusions from others that address *their* interpretation of what the facts mean. But as with the questions you've just asked, the conclusions you come across (even your own) should *also* be subjected to the same kind of inquisition as to whether the conclusions are sound and hold up.

The first few questions should address the structure of the conclusion, whether it comes from a sound basis in reasoning. A second set of questions addresses instead the quality of the conclusions and supporting arguments. We can see this through the same example of our Keynesian economics model:

What are the issues and conclusions of Keynesian economics? This question addresses the foundation of the theory—the problem it was trying to solve—and what the answers are.

What are the reasons for your conclusions? A well-worded conclusion will list out the facts being used to support it. This question identifies what those facts are. And you better separate facts from anecdotes or *feelings.*

What assumptions are you using in your theory? If there are any variable factors being used when the conclusion is formed, it's important to ferret them out. For example, the Keynesian model specifically addresses economic depression, so an assumption might be "assuming the economy has declined by 85% over the preceding year."

The next two questions seek to expose the shortcomings of thought that may have compromised the finding of the conclusions:

Are there fallacies in the reasoning? This question seeks out any inaccuracies, mistakes, or outright falsehoods in any of the reasons given. For example, the original conclusion could have been based on incorrect economic data from the 1930s. It's a different way of playing devil's advocate and trying to understand opposing stances or conclusions.

How good is the evidence? This is how you check that the supporting facts behind the conclusion are airtight, from legitimate sources, and not discolored by bias or misinformation. Did they use statistics from the U.S. Department of Labor or someone's propagandistic personal blog?

There's a chance that these questions might raise even *more* questions instead of answering all your inquiries. But again, that's the main point of this line of interrogation: to create a three-dimensional view of the topic you're investigating and not just stop at the first answer that looks "certain." Being certain is not the same as being right. In self-learning, you need to tune out the forced arguments borne from someone who just wants them to be true and focus on the real evidence and fact. Facts, in fact, are not enough for effective learning.

Researching from Scratch

The first step in learning anything is research: the step-by-step process of reading and analyzing materials relevant to your chosen field of interest. This is especially true when it is self-guided. But before we can understand and synthesize, we must *find* what we will be studying. It's a process that isn't inherently difficult, but many minefields exist that can derail your learning.

There is no shortage of information about almost everything, and we have better access to data and facts than we ever have before. But the sheer amount of information we have can make us forget about how to research effectively. How can we steer clear of questionable sources and make sure our research will bear fruit?

Research is a gradual process. It's methodical and investigative. These five steps of research, if executed thoughtfully and correctly, will give you what you need to gain mental command over a new topic. It's important to hit all five steps without skipping any. You'll be able to understand a concept, issue, or problem from a variety of angles and approaches.

We'll go through a thorough example after describing these steps to illustrate just what each step entails.

1. Gather information. The first step is to retrieve as much data about a topic as you possibly can. Collect anything and everything from as wide a range of sources as you can manage.

At this early stage of research, don't be too discriminating. Get as much as you can from wherever you can find it. Think what it would be like if you searched on Google about a certain topic, got 10 pages or more of results, and clicked on every single link. The point isn't to get immediate answers; it's to get an initial, panoramic overview of the subject you're investigating. So don't be too restrictive—open the floodgates. Organize the information you gather into general topics, arguments, and opinions. You might find that you are more confused after this stage than when you started—that's fine and natural. What's important is that you have everything in front of you, from shallow to deep and from correct to dubious.

2. Filter your sources. Now that you've got all the information you need, it's time to identify what your sources are, what kind of information they present, and whether it's good or not. This step could reduce the amount of information you'll study by 75% or even more.

Every information outlet has a different intent and approach over the subject matter it discusses. Some concentrate on hard and straight data. Some offer narrative accounts or anecdotes relating to the subject, while others offer editorial opinions or theories. Some sources are official agencies or authorities in your chosen field, while others are trade papers, media, groups, or associations who are interested in it. Some are simply blogs of opinionated people who have taken an interest in a particular topic with no expertise or common sense. And yes, some are "fake news."

Your goal here is to draw out the good sources and disregard the bad ones. A good source backs up its arguments and ideas with solid data, confirmable truth, and careful examination. A bad source is generally more interested in persuading through emotions and hyperbole and might rely on misleading or utterly wrong data to do so.

Don't confuse anecdote with evidence, even if there are multiple anecdotes. After all, that's how every single old wives' tale was started.

At this stage, you'll start noticing some divisions in the research you've collected. You'll see certain sources' tendencies and inclinations. You'll get a sense of which are the most popular or common outlooks (the majority), which are the rarer or more unusual viewpoints (the minority), and which ones are straight-up crazy ramblings from the minds of lunatics (the crackpots). You'll be able to divide up the sources and retain the ones that are most reliable and helpful.

3. Look for patterns and overlap. As you're viewing and reviewing all your source material, you'll begin to notice recurring topics, stances, and ideas. Certain points will crop up more frequently, and some will only appear once, seemingly randomly. You'll start getting a better idea of the primary points, secondary points, and boundaries of the subject you're looking into. You'll also be able to build bridges between parallel ideas and points of overlap.

Here you'll be able to identify the major components of your topic and the most prevalent thoughts and beliefs. Generally, the best sources will talk about the same things, so when that happens, you can safely assume they're the most important parts of your subject. When you see a point repeated by multiple sources, it's a good sign that you should consider it a major point or theme. Likewise, if you see things rarely mentioned by notable people in the field or that don't fit into the prevalent views, you know it's probably not something that moves the needle or is too new to be considered valuable.

This isn't to say less common or alternative points of view are necessarily wrong—they aren't. But use your better judgment. If only one isolated source is making a certain assertion, even if they have "disciples" who agree with all they say, there's a much higher chance that they're discussing something that's not really true or at least not very important.

You should understand what the main points and arguments are (and why), as well as a few of the minor ones, by the end of this step. Getting through this stage alone may qualify you as an expert relative to others, and it's common that most people stop their journey and education here. But if you stop here, you risk falling prey to *confirmation bias* and not knowing what you don't know.

4. Seek dissenting opinions. By this point, you'll no doubt have a theory or opinion in mind. You'll also have whittled down your sources to support that. So now's the time to look for sources that disagree with you. This is a hugely important step. Without knowing the full extent of opposing arguments, you won't have the complete picture that you need to understand the issue. No matter how convinced you are, try to find one.

Don't be afraid to question your own viewpoints by playing devil's advocate. If there's a minor quibble you have about your theory, this is the point where you indulge your imagination. Imagine all possible scenarios and circumstances where your theory might be put to the test.

Finding dissenting opinions is an important step in avoiding the all-too-common plague of confirmation bias—our human tendency to hear and see only what we want to hear and see. This is when someone dearly wants for a certain thing to be true, so they reject any solid evidence that it's false and only accept information that confirms their beliefs. That leads them to cherry-pick data that supports their point and ignore hard proof that disproves it. Confirmation bias is not objective, so it has no place in actual research. To combat it, give the voice of the opposition clear and full attention.

At this point, you may arrive at a conclusion that's been put through the paces. You have sophistication and nuance. The point is legitimate and not clouded by fallacies, misunderstanding, or disinformation. You'll comprehend your own beliefs more fully and understand why others may have different ideas. You'll be able to articulate precisely why you believe what you believe.

5. Put it all together. This is the point where you make your statement—only after you've considered all the above, rather than "shooting first and asking questions later." This is a point of clarity for you. You can explain all aspects of the topic or issue you're talking about. Write, speak, outline, or mind-map confidently about your new area of knowledge. Here's an easy way to think about how you summarize your expertise: put everything together to show

how you understand the whole situation, including the small and nuanced points: "X, Y, and Z because... *however,* A, B, and C because..." If you can't do this with certainty, you may need to go back a step or two in the process.

Let's show an example that illustrates all these steps at work and with at least a clear path for anyone who wishes to be an expert on a certain topic. For the sake of description, let's say you have a deep and driving need to become an expert in the *protest movements of the 1960s.*

Gather your info. Accumulate all the information you can without discrimination: history books, news articles, biographies, blogs, History Channel videos, websites, Congressional minutes, newsreels—anything. You're just herding in all the info you can at this stage. Any information is good information at this point. Use all mediums at your disposal. Don't forget to start your organization immediately by grouping and categorizing thoughts and opinions.

Filter your sources. Do you have news clippings from established sources like *The New York Times* or *Time* magazine? Are the stories verifiable? Do your biographies and nonfiction books provide meaningful information that's backed up, or are they thought pieces that don't rely on much data at all? Are the blogs you're looking at dependably referenced, or are they sloppily put together and filled with hyperbole? Are you actually just watching *Drunk History?* This point is where you use your discrimination and decide what sources are worth listening to (even if they have rare arguments) and what sources you should ditch (even if they parrot popular stances). Sorry to say it, but some opinions are worth more than others.

Look for patterns. Examine your sources for repeated mentions or descriptions of similar events—say, the Civil Rights Act, the assassination of JFK, the 1968 Democratic convention. Look for similar trends across varied eras: economic status, unemployment rates, election results, specific gatherings, or protests. The more often a certain event or trend appears in your review, the more likely it is to have been truly impactful on the subject. Examine all the views you can find: majority opinion, minority opinion, and even the crackpot ideas. Finding repeated patterns will give you a more three-dimensional view of the landscape.

Seek dissenting opinions. Hopefully by now you've formed a working thesis; now you put it to the test by finding well-reasoned opposing viewpoints. Ideally, some of your filtered reading material contains at least one counter-argument that has rationally constructed viewpoints. Alternately, doing a (very careful) Google search might produce some results. Weigh these dissenting opinions against your argument and consider where you may need to adjust certain parts of your contentions. Assume that everyone believes whole-heartedly that they are correct, and you will be more open to seeking people's stances instead of shutting them down.

Dig into not only what that opinion is, but why it is held and the assumptions it is based on. Insert whatever conspiracy theory you may have heard through the grapevine about prominent assassinations, and you'll get the idea—why do those ideas exist and who do they benefit?

Put it all together. Whether you keep it private or publish it, summarize your discoveries and opinions and keep them closely available. Make sure you've accounted for as many viewpoints as you can from both supportive and opposing viewpoints. For example, you may feel that the protest movements of the '60s arose from a sincere desire for change but may have come across some opinions that said they were inside jobs coordinated by the government. Leave room for the dissenting conclusions of others—they'll give your final result more body and legitimacy. Remember "X, Y, and Z because... *however,* A, B, and C because..."

The Skill of Self-Discipline

When I was young, a peer named Damon was strong in high school mock court tournaments. These are competitions in which you pretend to be part of a legal team arguing various cases in front of a judge, and in those days, if you won four cases in a row, you won the district championship.

Before he got into mock tournaments, Damon wasn't so interested in the law. He was more into basketball. But once he found out he was really good at it in high school, he decided he'd go to law school after he graduated college. At university he'd always talk about his ambition to be a lawyer, arguing huge cases that would impact society with his trademark wit and cunning.

Years later I ran into Damon at a local café. I asked him about his law ambitions and he turned a little sour. "I gave up. I underestimated just how much work and competition there was going to be. I was really looking forward to it. But after a few months of law school, I got nervous at how much of my life it was going to consume and how insurmountable all the work was, so I just backed out. Now my life is a lot calmer, but there's nothing going on. I'm wondering if I should have given it more of a chance."

We've loaded you up with a bunch of tools in this chapter—frameworks, goal-setting tips, scheduling suggestions, and ways to reorient your intellectual approach and make meaningful investigations into your subject matter. With all this information, at first glance you might get discouraged and think the whole process of self-education is, well, insurmountable.

And you would be exactly right. You're taking on a subject with which you're at least partially unfamiliar and going after it from scratch, with no outside force to help guide you. I'm not going to sugar-coat it: this won't be easy. You shouldn't underestimate just how much of a tough job this is going to be.

But why else would you want to do it? There are going to be moments in this process when you're not going to know where to go next. This not knowing will make you feel uneasy and undirected.

At times you'll feel like a juggler running out of hands. You'll be saturated with information. You won't know exactly how to connect all the dots and make the pieces fit. There will be concepts that you won't be able to grasp immediately. You'll have several plates spinning in the air and you won't know what's going to happen to them until they fall to the ground.

You'll probably want to quit. If you don't, you'll at least ask yourself if all this uncertainty is really worth the trouble in the end. You might feel this way more than once.

Then, at some point, probably when you least expect it, you'll hear that first "clink" in your head—and something will finally make *sense* to you.

This is going to happen.

But before it does, you're going to have to go through the beginning of the process. And with very few exceptions, beginnings kind of suck. You may start out with confidence and resolve and even get through a couple of points in the beginning with those feelings intact. Then, sometime when you feel you're supposed to make a great leap forward, you'll run into a mental roadblock. You'll feel anxious and doubtful.

When this *does* happen, just remember this: you didn't sign up for this to quit only part of the way through. You committed to the long term. You committed to the greater vision. You're thinking about zooming out and understanding that the present moment will always be a blip, whether positive or negative.

That's why it's important to keep the long view in mind when you're going through troublesome moments in self-learning. Your moments of anxiety will pass. It's all temporary.

Admittedly, we're not used to keeping the long view in our minds. We're more conditioned to deal with what's right in front of us, to take care of the most immediate items. In that view, fears and worries have unusual power: they're right there in the moment, and we feel them more acutely. Disappointment and disillusionment happen in everyone's lives, especially when we're working to make ourselves better. Those active negative emotions are present and certain—and the future that we're trying to improve isn't certain at all.

Keeping an eye on your long-term goals, though, will help you power through these negative emotions. When they hit, just acknowledge them, validate their reality, and call up the reasons why you're undertaking this endeavor: for the long term. Then move ahead.

Failure isn't to make you stop what you're doing—it's supposed to redirect you and encourage you to find a new way to go. The way that we prove ourselves is through rising to challenges that are always going to be presented to us.

What long-term thinking teaches us is that all these individual moments of terror over the uncertain future are temporary. They're not going to last. By keeping focused on that goal line, no matter how far off it is, those anxious moments will lose their power over time. They'll all eventually feel like exactly what they really are: temporary setbacks and minor exercises you need to go through to get where you're going.

One of two things will happen if you adopt the long game and acknowledge that the pain won't last: you'll either get used to the discomfort or the discomfort will dissipate. In either scenario, the anxiety will lose its power over you.

In a similar vein, you need to build *confusion endurance*. This confusion may come as a result of not knowing where to start, being perplexed at how to attack a problem, having a muddied view of what you're trying to achieve, wondering what resources are available and relevant to the task, and the like. Confusion endurance is all about being able to stay with a task and persisting instead of abandoning it when things get too difficult. It's about being able to persevere when you have the uncertainty and confusion of juggling multiple balls and not knowing where they will all land. It's the feeling of coming to a fork in the road with 10 paths and having to analyze each path.

Say you're standing in the middle of a messy room filled with boxes upon boxes of clutter to move and organize. It's an uncomfortable feeling to be surrounded by essentially chaos. You'll need to get creative with organizing the interior of the room in order to have enough space for everything you need to store inside it. If you don't have the ability to endure the chaos created by the mountain of disorganized stuff around you, you'll never stay with the task long enough to figure out a viable solution.

You'll need sufficient confusion endurance to withstand the initial disarray you're faced with, as well as the personal bewilderment you may feel from not knowing where to start or how to get the task done.

The bottom line is to remember that by taking on self-learning, you're doing something that is uniquely rewarding that only some of us ever do. It will impact your life and your confidence in exponentially positive ways. It'll be hard, it'll be frustrating, and it'll be a while. But embrace the uncertainty and the challenge and keep the long view uppermost in mind. When you finally get to where you want to go, all those obstacles will look like anthills in retrospect, and you'll know you're the better for them.

Concepts Before Facts, Understanding Before Memory

Researcher Roger Säljö found in 1979 that we tend to view the act of learning in several ways, but it can generally be boiled down into two rough categories: *surface* learning and *deep* learning. Surface learning relates to gaining knowledge, facts, and memorization; deep learning refers to abstracting meaning and understanding reality.

The use of the words "surface" and "deep" might imply that the latter is better in all situations than the former, but that's not always true. Some things are best learned by memorization rather than additionally searching for some "meaning" to contextualize those things. If I gave you a list of 30 random items and asked you to remember them, it probably wouldn't help to ransack your brain trying to find a pattern or relationship between each item. It would waste your time when the task at hand is simple information retention. And you would ultimately perform just fine on a test if you were to optimize for surface learning.

But more often than not, rote memorization serves to isolate facts rather than connect them. It establishes facts as single pieces of information, and without a grounding context or relationship to a greater concept, it doesn't anchor what you learn. Sometimes this is fine, but as a consequence, what you learn slips out of your short-term memory quite easily.

The overwhelming majority of things that can be learned have some kind of pattern—hidden or obvious. These patterns, typically, are what you most care about learning. Without these patterns, frankly, what you learn wouldn't be useful anyway. Patterns make concepts useful. Without them, concepts have very limited or temporary relevance and would therefore not be important to study in the first place.

A typical course of study contains a mix of big ideas with few details. In that setting, it's always the best idea to start with the big ideas—the overarching concepts that link the little details together.

The primary reason is that many small details take on a random quality at first, but when seen through the lens of the larger concept, they fit together and form a context. That makes them easier for the brain to recognize and remember.

In fact, you can often forgo a lot of memorization, because the concepts themselves often serve to explain the facts. Instead of attempting to memorize by rote means, following the concept through to its conclusion will reveal the facts as you go along. Like subheadings in an outline, they fall into place under the appropriate headings—it's a logical progression. If you understand the governing principles around something, the facts follow organically.

For example, if you were studying about the history of Miranda rights in the United States, you could memorize all the key players: the Supreme Court Justices, the lawyers, and the names of the plaintiffs and defendants. You could memorize the dates in the case. You could memorize the vote counts from all the courts involved in the suit and the appeals. You could memorize the names of cases that came afterward. You could even write down the contents of the Miranda rights ("You have the right to remain silent," etc.).

None of those facts would have any relevance by themselves, and we'd have no reason to keep them in memory. Emphasizing the larger concepts surrounding the Miranda rule—defendant's rights, police procedure, or landmark Supreme Court cases—help to funnel the facts as they come up. In this context, the brain is more likely to retain the information it actually needs to know about the subject. You would be able to essentially predict the facts with a reasonable degree of accuracy once you understand the underlying concepts and how they interact.

This is known as *concept learning*. It shows us how to categorize and discriminate items according to certain critical attributes. It entails pattern recall and integration of new examples and ideas. And rather than being a mechanical technique of grinding memorization, concept learning is something that must be constructed and cultivated.

Using Concept Learning in Daily Life. Applying the concept method to learning and developing new skills, even outside of the classroom or study hall environment, can help derive new meaning and, by logical extension, even improve how we perform certain tasks or jobs.

Cooking is an easy example. Standard practice is that learning a new recipe involves following a list of ingredients and a set of instructions. If you're making a tomato sauce for pasta, you can look up a popular recipe on the Internet and have it nearby as you prepare it. You can repeat this exercise as often as you like, and eventually you'll probably know the steps well enough to repeat it without a guide.

But understanding the *point* of each step isn't something that comes through in the instructions. They generally don't say *why* you sweat onions and garlic first, *why* you bring the sauce to a boil, or *why* you let it simmer for a time. Understanding that sweating the onions and garlic builds a flavor base, that boiling the sauce distributes the ingredients, and that simmering them bonds the flavors together gives you a better handle on the process of your preparation.

Most importantly, understanding those concepts makes it easier to recognize and use the techniques in other, completely different dishes: soups, chili, gravy, and even basic broth and stock. Going even further, learning the particulars of the exact scientific processes could open the door to *entirely* different foods that aren't liquid-based—in other words, any food you can think of. If you simply know which flavors tend to conflict and which tend to complement, you'll be way ahead of the chef who memorizes recipes.

This template is sneakily easy to replicate. A small business owner figuring a tax budget is better served knowing the concepts of taxation and how they're distributed. A musician who understands how rhythm works in the context of a song better knows how to program a drum machine. A chess player gets more mileage from comprehending the differences between overall strategies rather than learning where each piece can move. Even a clothes launderer makes fewer mistakes and ruins less clothing by learning how cold water and hot water affect colors in variant ways.

You can learn the particulars of any task and even perform it suitably a few times. But knowing the principles and ideas that link them together is a more effective way to preserve and retain those facts or skills. When the time comes to learn something new, you may very well be able to frame that new knowledge with concepts you've already nailed down.

Learning heuristics is very similar to the act of concept learning (Barsalou, 1991, 1992). Heuristics describes a pattern of thought or behavior that organizes categories of information and the relationships among them. It takes our preconceived notions or ideas of the world and uses them as a means for interpreting and classifying new information.

For example, there are ways you might act at a birthday party that you wouldn't at a funeral (and, we'd hope, the other way around). The "codes" you follow for how you'd handle and behave in each situation, and any other occasions, are ordered within a heuristic. Establishing and understanding the heuristic rules for whatever you're about to learn is always helpful. In any case, keep concepts and understanding at the forefront, because they can often fill in the blanks for you and enable you to learn more in less time.

The Right Mindset

This last point brings the book to a neat end, as it articulates on principles laid out in the first chapter. What you end up learning is what you believe you will end up learning.

In other words, this speaks to the confidence, motivation, and entire mindset that you bring with you to each new day.

Dr. Carol Dweck of Stanford University has studied attitudes toward learning for decades, as covered in her book *Mindset: The New Psychology of Success.* Dweck determined that most people adhere to one of two mindsets: fixed or growth.

People with the fixed mindset believe that talent and intelligence are inborn genetic traits. You either have talent or you don't. You were either born with intelligence or you weren't. You can either learn French or you can't. There's nothing you can do that will change that fact, because it's just your fate. You can imagine how this might affect your efforts and attitudes toward self-learning.

Those with the growth mindset, on the other hand, believe that talent, intelligence, and capability can be developed as one grows. Through work, effort, and struggle, a person can *become* talented or intelligent. To the growth mindset, failure isn't fatal;

it's just another step on the learning curve. If there is effort, there will be *some* change and improvement, leading to *a lot*. It's just a longer process.

Dweck found that people with the fixed mindset tended to focus their endeavors on tasks with high chances of success, which came from the desire to "look smart." They steered away from jobs where any kind of struggle was involved. They avoided obstacles, ignored criticism, and felt threatened by others' successes. They also tended to not try new things or experiment because they felt failure was imminent.

People with the growth mindset, Dweck asserted, were more open and embraced challenges. They believed that tenacity and effort could change the outcome of their learning. They persisted through barriers, listened to critical feedback from others, and used other people's successes as inspiration and learning opportunities.

How you interpret challenges, setbacks, and criticism is your choice. You can interpret them through a fixed mindset and say you don't have the talent or ability to succeed, or you can use the growth mindset to use those obstacles as openings to stretch yourself, ramp up your strategic efforts, and expand your skills. You might be able to guess which is more conducive to accelerated learning and exposure to anything new—which one do you think is a mistake in learning?

Dweck's most revelatory research explored how these mindsets are created. Not surprisingly, it likely starts early in our lives. There's no intention here to skew to Sigmund Freud's perspective that everything we are was a result of our childhood experiences, but there are undoubtedly more connections than meet the eye.

In one seminal study, Dweck and her colleagues offered four-year-olds a choice: they could either redo an easy jigsaw puzzle or try a harder one.

Children who showed fixed mentalities stayed on the safe side and chose the simpler puzzles that would affirm the abilities they already had, whereas the kids with growth mentalities considered the mere *option* strange: why would someone want to do the same puzzle over and over and not learn anything new?

The fixed-mindset children were focused on results that would guarantee success and give them the appearance of being smart. The growth-minded kids wanted to stretch their abilities. For them, the definition of success was *becoming* smarter. Ultimately, the growth-minded kids did what they wanted to do because they weren't necessarily concerned about possibilities or failure.

Dweck's study got even more interesting. She brought adults into the brainwave lab at Columbia University to study how their brains behaved as they answered questions and received feedback.

The fixed-mindset kids were only interested in feedback that reflected their present abilities. They turned a deaf ear to information that might have helped them learn and improve their performance.

Strikingly, they showed no interest in hearing the right answer to a question they had gotten wrong—they had already labeled their answer as a failure and had no further use for it.

People with a growth mindset, though, paid keen attention to information that would help them gain knowledge and develop new skills. For them, there was no shame in getting the answer wrong, and the explanation of the right answer was welcomed as a great help in their development. The growth-mindset kids' priorities were learning—not the binary ego trap of success or failure. What manifests in childhood can stay with us for an entire lifetime if not addressed.

Fortunately, no matter how deeply a fixed mindset is ingrained in a person, it doesn't have to be a permanent condition as they might believe. Mindsets are malleable and can be taught. It turns out old dogs *can* learn new tricks.

Dweck and her colleagues developed a technique they called "growth mindset intervention." The usage of the word "intervention" might make it sound like a mid-life crisis, but the beauty of the idea is how minor the adjustments really are. Small changes in communication—even in the most innocuous comments—can have long-lasting implications for a person's mindset. This goes for how you communicate with yourself as well.

One key area of focus in this technique is the nature of praise. Complimenting someone's process ("I really appreciate how you struggled with that problem") rather than their innate trait or talent ("You're so clever") is an easy but powerful way to promote the growth mindset.

Talent praise only reinforces the notion that success or failure rests on an inborn, unchangeable, static, and stagnant trait. Process praise applauds the effort and work—the *action* that's taken to get to the next step. You want to reinforce the idea that talent is unimportant, whereas effort is everything.

It's true that there are polyglots among us who seem to be able to learn new languages within days. But they are the vast minority; everyone else who has ever learned a new language struggled for months or years, and still probably has an accent and poor grammar. Yet they believed they could, and that hiccups were part of the journey.

This is far from a book on mindset, but all the techniques that we've discussed will be rendered useless if you don't believe that they can deliver you to the outcome you want. Self-learning starts with telling yourself that you are exactly the type of person to excel at it, simply because you want to do it—not based on your past, perceived talents or shortcomings, or arbitrarily limiting beliefs. Whether you believe you can or cannot self-learn, you will be correct. Start slow, do the work, and you will be surprised at where you find yourself in a short amount of time.

Takeaways:

- There are certain skills and habits you must cultivate in your quest for self-learning and self-education. Many of these stem from the simple fact that with no one else to regulate you, you must do it yourself. Again, the theme that you must be both student and teacher rears its ugly head.

- First, plans, schedules, and goals should all figure heavily into your self-learning. In fact, they should be one of the first things you create—all three of them. Take a page from Benjamin Franklin (twice) and implement a daily schedule that simplifies your decision-making, as well as a plan and schedule for accomplishing your goals. Make sure your goals are challenging enough to be motivating but not so impossible as to create discouragement. Think SMART.

- Information itself is not going to teach you. You must have a dialogue with the material you discover and interact with it in a way that makes up for not having a stimulating teacher or professor. You must *pull* information out. You can accomplish this through asking critical and probative questions—the goal is to gain understanding, context, and perspective, not to seek a correct answer. As long as you focus on the overall purpose of finding a nuanced and three-dimensional view of a topic, your questions will be well-guided.

- Research. It's not as simple as going to the library and checking out a book or consulting Wikipedia and calling it a day. In the same vein as the previous point on *pulling* information, you must ensure that you are finding a complete and thorough understanding of a topic through five steps: gather, filter, find patterns, seek dissent, and put it all together.

- Self-discipline is needed in heavy doses because self-learning is not innately a pleasurable pursuit. It's work. And it can induce anxiety, stress, and discouragement that ultimately lead to giving up. Look at your moments of anxiety and view them as temporary and passing. The pain won't last forever, you'll grow accustomed to it, or you'll solve it. These are all acceptable outcomes to the occasionally painful process you must endure.

- Deep learning and surface learning are different. Deep learning comes from understanding concepts and patterns, and often, then supersedes the need for shallow, surface learning. The same parallel exists with regard to trying to memorize something, versus trying to understand it. If you simply prioritize concepts and understanding, you'll be able to fill in the blanks of specific information by yourself.

- Before you self-learn, your mindset must allow it happen. You can either possess a *growth* mindset or a *fixed* mindset—the former recognizes that growth will occur with sufficient effort (growth=effort), while the latter believes that growth is not a function of effort, rather luck/fate/innate talent (growth=luck). The growth mindset is what allows you to learn effectively because it espouses the belief that you can do it. Whether you can or cannot, you are correct. All the techniques in the world won't make a difference in your learning if you don't think it will ultimately happen for you.

Summary Guide

Chapter 1. Principles of Self-Learning

- Self-learning is a pursuit that isn't new, but what's new is how possible and attainable it is. The world is your oyster, courtesy of the Internet, and we have the ability to learn anything we want these days. Traditional learning has some positive aspects, but it also severely limits our approach toward education and how we seek to enrich ourselves. To combat this, we must first take a cue from autodidacts and understand the difference in mindset between reading and regurgitation and intellectual curiosity.

- The learning success pyramid accurately lays out the three aspects of learning, two of which are typically neglected and thus serve as enormous barriers for most people. First, you must have confidence in your ability to learn, otherwise you will grow discouraged and hopeless. Second, you must be able to self-regulate your impulses, be disciplined, and focus when it matters— you can lead a horse to water, but you can't make him drink. Third comes learning, which is where most people tend to start—to their detriment. Learning is more than picking up a book and reading, at least psychologically.

- Self-motivation is related to self-regulation. It's an essential aspect of self-learning because there is no educator to impose rigidity upon you— just yourself. You are both the teacher and the student, and that comes with the task of self-motivation. There are three main aspects of intrinsic motivation to keep yourself moving toward your goal of self-learning: autonomy, mastery, and purpose/impact. The intangibles tend to be far more powerful than what you would traditionally consider motivating.

Chapter 2. Interaction with Information

- Interaction with information—in other words, how to take something that's on the page and screen, understand it, and make it usable to yourself at a later time. That's learning in a nutshell, but there are best practices you should embrace outside of the traditional classroom setting.
- First is the SQ3R method. Use it. It stands for survey, question, read, recite, review. This is not just a process for attacking a book, but rather a plan for attacking entire disciplines and fields— and whatever you are trying to learn for yourself. Most people will use some elements of the SQ3R method, such as the read and review portion, but without the other elements, deeper comprehension is rarer and more difficult.
- Second is Cornell notes. Use them. Cornell notes split your note-taking into three parts: taking notes, writing cues, and summarizing. In this way, you create your own study guide, with the ability to go into as much detail as you want on command. The fact that you've gone

through the information three times also doesn't hurt.

- Finally, self-explanation. Do it. When we are forced to try to explain concepts through self-inquiry, we will quickly discover what we do know and what we don't know at all. These are called blind spots, and they are far more common than you might like to think. Can you explain why the sky is blue or how gravity works? Probably not off the top of your head, even though you think you understand those concepts. The Feynman technique is an offshoot of self-explanation that helps find blind spots as well, with an added component of using an analogy to explain what you think you know.

Chapter 3. Read Faster and Retain More

- This chapter is geared toward imparting how to read faster and also retain more information at the same time. It sounds like a tall task, but it's unlikely you've learned much about reading since when you were learning the alphabet—that is to say, not much. There are a few important aspects to reading faster.

- You must stop subvocalizations. This is when you mentally read words out loud. You can think and process faster than you can read out loud. This means instead of sounding out and pronouncing words, you must imagine their meaning in their place. It's a tough habit to break.

- Second, you must train your eyes. After all, each eye has six muscles that control its movements. You must train your eyes in two ways: to move less and to look wider with peripheral vision.

- Third, you must learn how to strategically skim by avoiding useless words, focusing on important words, and ignoring words at the edge of the pages.

- Finally, you must learn how your focus and attention works in regard to reading. Give it the respect it deserves and take scheduled breaks, make games to read faster, and eliminate distractions.

- How do you read a book? A final section details the four levels of reading as articulated by author Mortimer Adler. The levels are elementary, inspectional, analytical, and syntopical. Most of us only get through the first two levels and don't engage with the material and have a conversation with it. That's where deep, true comprehension comes from.

Chapter 4. Skills and Habits to Teach Yourself Anything

- There are certain skills and habits you must cultivate in your quest for self-learning and self-education. Many of these stem from the simple fact that with no one else to regulate you, you must do it yourself. Again, the theme that you must be both student and teacher rears its ugly head.
- First, plans, schedules, and goals should all figure heavily into your self-learning. In fact, they should be one of the first things you create—all three of them. Take a page from Benjamin Franklin (twice) and implement a daily schedule

that simplifies your decision-making, as well as a plan and schedule for accomplishing your goals. Make sure your goals are challenging enough to be motivating but not so impossible as to create discouragement. Think SMART.

- Information itself is not going to teach you. You must have a dialogue with the material you discover and interact with it in a way that makes up for not having a stimulating teacher or professor. You must *pull* information out. You can accomplish this through asking critical and probative questions—the goal is to gain understanding, context, and perspective, not to seek a correct answer. As long as you focus on the overall purpose of finding a nuanced and three-dimensional view of a topic, your questions will be well-guided.

- Research. It's not as simple as going to the library and checking out a book or consulting Wikipedia and calling it a day. In the same vein as the previous point on *pulling* information, you must ensure that you are finding a complete and thorough understanding of a topic through five steps: gather, filter, find patterns, seek dissent, and put it all together.

- Self-discipline is needed in heavy doses because self-learning is not innately a pleasurable pursuit. It's work. And it can induce anxiety, stress, and discouragement that ultimately lead to giving up. Look at your moments of anxiety and view them as temporary and passing. The pain won't last forever, you'll grow accustomed to it, or you'll solve it. These are all acceptable outcomes to the occasionally painful process you must endure.

- Deep learning and surface learning are different. Deep learning comes from understanding concepts and patterns, and often, then supersedes the need for shallow, surface learning. The same parallel exists with regard to trying to memorize something, versus trying to understand it. If you simply prioritize concepts and understanding, you'll be able to fill in the blanks of specific information by yourself.

- Before you self-learn, your mindset must allow it happen. You can either possess a *growth* mindset or a *fixed* mindset—the former recognizes that growth will occur with sufficient effort (growth=effort), while the latter believes that growth is not a function of effort, rather luck/fate/innate talent (growth=luck). The growth mindset is what allows you to learn effectively because it espouses the belief that you can do it. Whether you can or cannot, you are correct. All the techniques in the world won't make a difference in your learning if you don't think it will ultimately happen for you.

Manufactured by Amazon.ca
Bolton, ON

28731211R00118